P9-DTE-447

IN THE FOOTSTEPS OF MOSES

IN THE FOOTSTEPS OF MOSES

LEON AMIEL
PUBLISHER

MOSHE PEARLMAN

PHOTOGRAPHY BY DAVID HARRIS

GENERAL EDITOR MORDECAI RAANAN
DESIGN CONSULTANT GAD ULMAN

Copyright © 1973 by NATEEV-printing & publishing enterprises ltd.
P.O.Box 6048, Tel-Aviv, Israel

De-Luxe Editions:

First Printing, January 1973
Second Printing, July 1973
Third Printing, December 1973
Fourth Printing, July 1974
Fifth Printing, June 1975
Sixth Printing, December 1975
Seventh Printing, July 1976

Paper-Back Editions:

First Printing, November 1973
Second Printing, June 1975
Third Printing, July 1976

Published in:

Israel, by Nateev and Steimatzky, Tel-Aviv
United States of America, by Leon Amiel Publisher
Switzerland, by Walter Verlag, Olten und Freiburg im Breisgau
France, by Editions Arthaud, Paris et Grenoble
Brazil, by Bloch Editores, Rio de Janeiro

ACKNOWLEDGMENTS and thanks are due to the following institutions and persons for having kindly permitted their exhibits to be photographed: Department of Antiquities and Museums, Ministry of Education and Culture, Jerusalem; Rockefeller Museum, pages 21, 130–31, 177; Israel Museum, pages 122, 184, 198; The Jewish National and University Library, Jerusalem, pages 152–53; The Library of St. Thoros, The Armenian Orthodox Patriarchate, Jerusalem, pages 64, 72, 116; U.S. Information Service, The Embassy of the U.S.A., Tel Aviv, page 69; The Pierpont Morgan Library, New York, N.Y., pages 181, 201; E. M. Cross, Jr., Harvard University, pages 126–27. Photographs by Uzi Paz, page 104; by Werner Braun, page 106; by other photographers, pages 13, 14–15, 25, 26–27, 125, 128.

Manufactured in Israel
by Nateev-printing and publishing enterprises ltd.

CONTENTS

FOREWORD

    BY PROFESSOR YIGAEL YADIN 7

1. THE REVOLUTIONARY

                    COURTIER 6

THE HEBREWS IN EGYPT   11

THE BABE IN THE RIVER   21

THE COURT OF PHARAOH   24

FUGITIVE IN THE DESERT   32

THE REVELATION   40

2. THE GREAT FREEDOM TREK 44

THE TWO BROTHERS   44

THE TRIBAL PATTERN   53

A FATEFUL MEETING   65

THE CALL TO RESISTANCE   68

THE FIRST PASSOVER   76

EXODUS   79

THE WATERS PART   84

CRISIS IN SINAI   95

MILITARY ENCOUNTER   105

ADMINISTRATIVE REFORM   108

3. THE LAW-GIVER 112

DECALOGUE ON THE MOUNT   112

COVENANT TREATIES   117

THE ORDINANCES   124

REBELLION   133

DRASTIC ACTION   136

4. MOULDING A NATION 140

THE LONG SOJOURN   141

INTELLIGENCE MISSION   143

AN ABORTIVE FORAY   147

THE NEW GENERATION   151

THE LAST LAP   154

MOSES' FAREWELL   160

5. THE PROMISED LAND 169

JOSHUA THE WARRIOR-LEADER   169

STRATAGEM IN BATTLE   176

THE ARCHAEOLOGICAL EVIDENCE 186

TRIBAL SETTLEMENT   187

THE CONFEDERACY   191

THE CHARISMATIC TWELVE   199

INDEX   221

AUTHOR'S NOTE

I thank Dr. Moshe Weinfeld, Senior Lecturer in Bible, Hebrew University,
Jerusalem, who read the manuscript and made valuable suggestions, particularly
on the covenant tradition in the ancient Near East dealt with in Chapter 3.
My thanks go also to Magen Broshi, Curator of the Shrine of the Book,
Israel Museum, Jerusalem, and to Ze'ev Yeivin, of the Israel government's
Department of Antiquities, for their help in the selection of the illustrations.

Jerusalem, January 1973   Moshe Pearlman

A momentous event occurred some thirty-two hundred years ago which was to affect the course of history for many peoples to this very day. This was the Exodus from Egypt of the Israelites and their conquest and settlement of the Promised Land.

In this grand human adventure, the name of one man, Moses, stands out as leader, commander and law-giver. The impact of the Exodus upon the lives of a great portion of the human race lay in its spiritual message, and also in its vital political consequences. Since those days, the Law of Moses and the Land of Israel became one inseparable entity, and the hallmark of the Jewish people.

Moshe Pearlman has succeeded in giving the general reader a clear and comprehensive account of this drama, where the professional historian, archaeologist or biblical scholar, in the absence of the complete historical facts, might well have been caught in the thickets of conflicting theories and his own biased views.

The author is not a newcomer to the historical and archaeological subjects of the biblical world. His books on the historical sites of Israel and on Jerusalem are still the most readable and accurate of their kind.

"In the Footsteps of Moses" is a fascinating narrative, beautifully illustrated, which offers the general reader the gist of the history of the Jewish people in their formative years.

Yigael Yadin
Professor of Archaeology
Hebrew University of Jerusalem

January 1973

1. THE REVOLUTIONARY COURTIER

He was born under sentence of death, yet he lived a full span, and more. He grew up amid the luxury of a royal court, yet he threw in his lot with slaves. Coddled and pampered by an absolute monarch, he joined the monarch's most persecuted victims. Trained in the strict tenets of a ritual conservatism, he became a revolutionary. Halting of speech he uttered words of sublime wisdom. In a world and a time of corruption, with little value placed on human life, he put forth a timeless and unexcelled code of ethics for the human race. Taken at birth from his people and their faith, he established their distinctive religion and moulded them into a nation.

This was Moses. He was to learn much and suffer much in his formative years, and undergo strange experiences, encounters and adventures before he emerged as a giant of his times, and of all times—Law-Giver, first and greatest of the Hebrew prophets, resistance leader and statesman, field commander and teacher.

The date of Moses' birth in Egypt is now placed by current historians and archaeologists at the beginning of the 13th century BC, a period when Egypt was already losing strength. Up to only a few years earlier, however, she had been the dominant power in the Middle East, commanding the greatest and most extensive imperial role she ever enjoyed, either before or since. She had held this proud position for two hundred and fifty years, from the middle of the 16th to the end of the 14th century BC. Now, as the 13th century opened, she had to vie with the Hittite empire in the north for hegemony of the region. (Both empires were to decline by the end of the century, and this would ease the Israelite settlement of the territory that lay between them, the land of Canaan.)

Nevertheless, Egypt was still a country of prestige and glory, boasting the highest material standards in the area, with artists, scribes, craftsmen, farmers, architects, engineers, administrators and men of affairs of extraordinary sophistication. Yet with all its splendour, the country was filled with vast

9

*the daughter of Pharaoh...
saw the basket... and lo,
the babe was crying... she
named him Moses*

(*Exodus 2:5, 6, 10*)

The infant Moses is taken from his floating
basket by the Egyptian princess. Scene
from the remarkable frescoes in the 244 AD
synagogue of Dura-Europos, the ancient
Babylonian town. The synagogue was discovered
at archaeological excavations in 1932.

human misery. The bulk of the Egyptian
population lived in squalor and only the few
could enjoy the product of Egypt's imagina-
tion, artistry and technical skills. At the head
of the State sat the all-powerful Pharaoh. At
the bottom were the slaves, for the most part
captives taken in battle. At a level just above
them were certain oppressed communities
from whom forced-labour gangs were drawn
to quarry stone, make bricks and build the
proud pharaonic cities, temples and monuments.

THE HEBREWS IN EGYPT

One such community were the Hebrews. Their
fortunes had indeed ebbed since the time,
early in the 16th century, when the Pharaoh's
principal adviser and Governor of Egypt had
been the young Hebrew, Joseph, son of the
Patriarch Jacob. He had brought his father
and brothers, together with their families,
from famine-ridden Canaan and settled them,
with the Pharaoh's blessing, in the Land of
Goshen. This district in northeastern Egypt
was bounded on the east by what is today the
Suez Canal. There the Hebrews lived as a

11

Then Pharaoh commanded..., 'Every son that is born to the Hebrews you shall cast into the Nile' (Exodus 1:22)

The Nile, the great African river which runs through Egypt and gives life to the country; but at the time of Moses' birth, it was a river of death, following the Pharaoh's decree that all new-born Hebrew males should be cast into its waters. Parts of it are so wide that it is sometimes called "The sea of the Nile".

tribal community, pasturing their flocks, and remembering, despite exposure to the idolatrous practices of the Egyptians, the covenant of their Patriarchs with the one invisible God.

Of their experiences during the three hundred years following the death of Joseph we know little beyond the bare biblical record that "the descendants of Israel [Jacob] were fruitful and increased greatly; they multiplied and grew exceedingly strong; so that the land was filled with them". (Ex. 1:7.) It is evident, however, that at some point during this period they suffered a catastrophic reverse. One feasible explanation given by some modern scholars is that this occurred early on, in the middle of the 16th century, with the ending of the Hyksos regime.

The Hyksos were a northern people (possibly from Syria) who, towards the end of the 18th century, thundered down through Canaan and invaded Egypt. The Egyptians at the time were riven by dynastic rivalries, and the Hyksos took advantage of this weakness. The invaders, moreover, were armed with powerful new weapons—the horse-drawn chariot and the composite bow—and soon overran the Egyptian defences. It took them another few decades to master the whole of the country, and for more than one hundred years the Hyksos ruled Egypt as well as a considerable western Asiatic empire. (Canaan was part of it, and archaeological excavations in Israel have brought to light considerable evidence of Hyksos rule, particularly the new type of fortifications. These were embankments of beaten-earth, to protect their large chariot concentrations, and similar embankments plus formidable masonry revetments as a base for the walls to defend their cities against another new weapon which became general during this period — the battering ram. An excellent example of such Hyksos fortifications are the well-preserved remains discovered in the mid–1950s by the excavations undertaken by Prof. Yigael Yadin at Hazor, in Galilee.)

The seat of Hyksos government was Avaris, a new capital which they founded at the northern edge of the Land of Goshen and close to the northeastern Egyptian frontier, well sited to control their imperial territories. Not until a hundred years later did the Egyptians begin

12

The pyramids, the royal tombs of the ancient Pharaohs, were constructed by huge armies of slaves. This is one of the three great pyramids of Gizeh, and stands 450 feet high on an almost square base of some 750 by 750 feet. The 5th century BC Greek historian Herodotus estimated that it took 100,000 slaves twenty years to build.

15

So they made the people of Israel serve with rigour...

It was from quarries like this
that the huge stones were
extracted by slave labour and used
for the construction of the pyramids.

their struggle for liberation, and not until about 1550 was Avaris captured and the Hyksos driven out. This heralded the dawn of Egypt's greatness.

It is suggested that Joseph's royal friend was probably a Hyksos ruler, and that Jacob and his family had settled in Goshen during the Hyksos regime. Thus, when the hated Hyksos had been overthrown, the new Egyptian kings would have dealt harshly with the Israelite and other foreign tribes who had been associated with the invaders. Hatred of the Israelites remained, and as Pharaoh followed Pharaoh, each seeking to outdo his predecessor in the construction of monumental buildings and cities, the Israelites became a royal reservoir for forced labour. Despite this, the Hebrews, still a "foreign" element, somehow managed to multiply and grow "exceedingly strong", thereby arousing an even deeper xenophobia among the Egyptians. By the time Moses was born, they were a community of State slaves in bond to a new Pharaoh "who did not know Joseph", and who "said to his people, 'Behold, the people of Israel are too many and too mighty for

16

Making mud bricks. This was one
of the tasks forced upon the
Israelite slaves, who had to
complete a heavy quota each day.

us'...." And so he "set taskmasters over them
to afflict them with heavy burdens; and they
built for Pharaoh store-cities, Pithom and
Raamses." (Ex. 1:11.)

The Pharaoh at this time is believed by
most modern scholars to have been Sethos I
(1309–1290 BC), son of Rameses I, founder of
the 19th Dynasty, and father of the redoutable
Rameses II (1290–1224). The city of Pithom
built by the Hebrew slaves was at the southern
edge of Goshen, to the west of Lake Timsah
and a few miles southwest of today's Ismailia.
Raamses, at the northern edge of Goshen, just
off Lake Manzala and southwest of today's
Port Said, was none other than the site of the
ancient Hyksos capital Avaris, and it was now
beginning to be rebuilt by the slaves at the
order of Sethos I. His son Rameses II completed the rebuilding of this city and renamed
it after himself, and as such, though in the
slightly altered form of Raamses, it appears in
Exodus. [Its name was changed to Tanis two
centuries later, and in Numbers (13:22) and
Psalms (78:12, 43) it is also referred to as
Zoan.]

Putting the Hebrews under a harsh bondage

17

The turquoise quarries at Serabit
el-Khadem on the eastern shore of the
Gulf of Suez where Semitic slaves
laboured for the ancient Egyptian
rulers, including the Pharaoh
who reigned at the time of the Exodus.

might have been considered sufficient expression of the Pharaoh's morbid hatred of this foreign community, with their strange customs and odd belief in an invisible God and their implicit rejection of the gods worshipped by the monarch. It was also highly profitable — for as long as they were alive; and it was general pharaonic policy to keep serfs alive. But xenophobia is often contradictory and always irrational, as the behaviour of leading xenophobes throughout history, right down to Hitler in our own day, has shown, and cruelty to the Hebrews was not enough. They had to be eliminated, even though this would mean losing a sizeable labour force. However, in order not to interfere with the immediate progress of his grandiose construction projects, the Pharaoh ordered the death not of the working adults but of all Hebrew male infants. This would guarantee the eventual annihilation of the community, the surviving women remaining servants and concubines to the Egyptians.

The royal edict accordingly went out that Hebrew midwives, when attending a birth, "if it is a son, you shall kill him". (Ex. 1:14.) The

Proto-Sinaitic inscription on the face of the rock (left) in the quarries of Serabit el-Khadem discovered in 1905. The text is Semitic, and is believed to have been written by one of the slave miners at the turn of the 15th century BC. Proto-Sinaitic is the first writing in the region to use the letter form as distinct from the pictorial (as in the hieroglyph, which used the figure of an object for a word or a sound), and is the progenitor of most existing alphabets. 16th century BC dagger (right) bearing proto-Sinaitic inscription discovered at archaeological excavations at Lachish (in the southern Judea of today).

20

midwives ignored the order, and when they were called to account they explained to the authorities that "the Hebrew women are not like the Egyptian women; for they are vigorous and are delivered before the midwife comes to them". The Pharaoh therefore entrusted the task to his own people, ordering them to cast new-born Hebrew males into the Nile.

THE BABE IN THE RIVER

It was at this time that a son was born to Amram and Jochebed of the tribe of Levi, the most observant of the tribes in their adherence to the Hebrew faith and avoidance of the pagan ways of the Egyptians. Jochebed promptly hid the child, and kept him hidden for three months, wondering all the while what she would do thereafter, for if he were spotted in public by an Egyptian inspector he would assuredly be taken and killed. She eventually evolved a plan which she would put into effect at the appropriate time. Thus it came about that "when she could hide him no longer she took for him a basket made of bulrushes, and daubed it with bitumen and

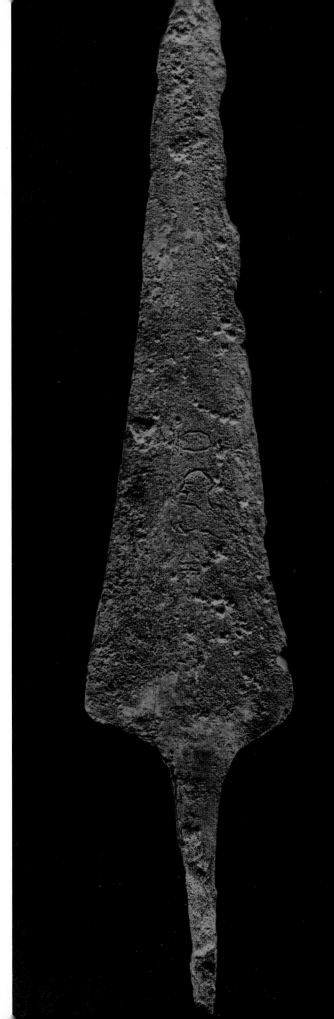

Temple to the Egyptian goddess Hathor (left)
at Serabit el-Khadem, established for
the Egyptian overseers of the Semitics slaves
who worked in the quarries. Hieroglyphic
inscriptions carved on stone (below) found
in this temple.

pitch; and she put the child in it and placed it among the reeds at the river's brink. And his sister stood at a distance, to know what would be done to him." (Ex. 2:3, 4.) It was her hope that the child would be picked up and taken into an Egyptian home, as the only way in which his life could be spared. His sister, Miriam, watchful on the bank, would see who was the foster-mother, establish contact, follow the child's progress, and perhaps eventually be able to retrieve him.

The foster-mother turned out to be the Pharaoh's daughter, who noticed the basket when she came down to the river to bathe. Though she realised that this must be "one of the Hebrews' children" and therefore condemned by her father, she seems to have been much taken with the infant, evidently holding it in her arms and cooing over it. Witnessing all this from the bank, Miriam approached the princess and offered to find her a wet-nurse for the baby. The princess agreed and Miriam went to fetch her mother. Jochebed thus nursed her own child for the Pharaoh's daughter, who adopted him and brought him up as one of the princes in her father's court. (The Hebrew for Moses is Moshe, and according to popular Hebrew etymology, he was given this name because it means "drawn forth from the water"; but scholars now agree that the name "Moses" is of Egyptian origin and means "child".)

THE COURT OF PHARAOH

Life at any royal court in any land and in any age is usually far removed from the life of the populace. In the court of Pharaoh, at that time, it was even more so, because of the monarch's need to demonstrate — as the moral source of his supreme authority — that he had been chosen by the gods. The phenomenal temples he caused to be erected, his sumptuous palaces with their opulent furnishings and appointments, his costly personal attire, were all designed to underline his unique status. But it was not only the luxury, the pomp, the stately ceremonial, the banqueting, the lavish arrangements for the hunt and other expensive pursuits which marked off the pharaonic pattern from the drab life of the common people. It was also that members of the court lived on a tight little royal island, cut off from

the public, aware of their existence but hardly aware of them as human beings. The lives of the slaves touched them not at all, though the product of slavery did. There was great excitement in the palace, for example, when the Pharaoh was told of an unusually large stone which had been spotted deep in the desert and ten thousand slaves were mobilised to extract and haul it. The episode is recorded in hieroglyphic inscriptions discovered at Wadi Hammamat glorifying the ruler: "My Majesty sent forth Amenemhat, the hereditary prince and vizier, chief of the works...in order to bring him back a block of precious stone worthy of reverence, the finest that is in the mountain... to make therefrom a sarcophagus...." The thoughts of the courtiers would have been centred wholly on the "block of precious stone", never on the wretches who had laboured to bring it in.

This, then, was the insulated world in which the boy Moses grew up. In one sphere, however, it was not insulated. Within the precincts of the palace, the Pharaoh conducted affairs of State, and as a young man Moses must have been present on some occasions when the

there arose a new king over Egypt...he said...'Behold, the people of Israel are too many' (*Exodus 1:8, 9*)

Statue of Rameses II, the Pharaoh at the time of the Exodus, in one of the three temples at Abu Simbel, on the west bank of the Nile in the province of Aswan. Rameses built these temples as a monument to himself and his deeds.

These four colossi, fashioned in the likeness of Rameses and 65 feet in height, flank the entrance to the principal temple which was discovered in 1812. It was carved out of the sandstone cliffs near the river edge, and the halls within contain scenes in coloured relief depicting outstanding events in the life of this Pharaoh.

Reeds at the edge of the river Nile. It was amidst such reeds that Jochebed hid the basket of bulrushes containing her infant son Moses, and it was there that he was spotted by Pharaoh's daughter when she came down to bathe.

ruler conducted investitures, received foreign ambassadors, heard reports from his own delegates and administrators, met with his advisers, consulted with his military men.

But perhaps more important for the princes than occasional attendance at such audiences were the frequent talks and daily contact with royal counsellors, chamberlains and other court officials, from whom they could absorb much of the background to the issues which came before the ruler. Moreover, if, for example, a commander were reporting privately to the Pharaoh on a military campaign, or presenting intelligence on threatening moves by a potential enemy, the commander's aide, waiting in the ante-chamber, would feel flattered to give the same information in an informal chat to an eager prince — who might become the future ruler. In the same casual way, princes could hear progress reports on construction projects initiated by the Pharaoh, how the work was organised, whether there was any trouble with the slaves and what steps were taken to deal with it.

It is thus reasonable to suppose that the young Moses was familiar with the power structure, the use of power and the manner in which it was wielded. He would have seen something of the conduct of affairs at the highest level and observed the patterns of diplomacy and the process of decision-making. On the technical plane, from top army commanders and from public works officials in charge of slave projects he would have picked up much information on logistics and the organisation and movement of large formations. We can imagine him, for example, with his singular gifts and character, cross-examining the aide of whoever was the prince "Amenemhat...chief of the works" in his day. How did they move "ten thousand slaves" over long distances? How many miles did they cover a day? What about food and water? Where and how did they bivouac? What devices did they use for hauling heavy weights?

Such questioning of officials in sundry spheres would have elicited much valuable data. Though he could hardly have conceived it at the time, he would be applying this knowledge in later years to a strange purpose, unique in history.

28

It is evident from what subsequently happened that while living as a young prince at Pharaoh's court, Moses must have maintained surreptitious contact with his real family. The likeliest go-between would have been Miriam. The girl was known to the princess, Moses' foster-mother, and was privy to her secret. At some stage she may have gained a closer intimacy with her by indicating that she was the sister of the infant. In making this disclosure, she would have run the risk of angering the princess, with dire consequences; but apparently the princess showed understanding. Later, when the youth was accounted ripe for it, Miriam may have been instructed by Jochebed her mother — who appears from the Bible to have been the strong personality in the family — to tell Moses who he was and how he came to be in the royal palace. She would no doubt have done so in the presence of the princess, for the immediate shock of the revelation would otherwise have sent the "prince" scurrying to his "mother" for confirmation. In every way, this daughter of Pharaoh seems to have been a most remarkable lady.

The news must have been shattering to the young Moses. But after he had assimilated it, he had clearly resolved to live with it and learn more, and at subsequent meetings with Miriam, perhaps arranged through the princess, he would have sought to hear what was happening to his people. His must have been an agonising youth, living as he did the outward life of a carefree prince yet carrying in his heart the knowledge of his origins and the anguish of his people.

The Bible is silent on this, proceeding directly from the story of his adoption as a babe to his dramatic encounter, as a young man, with slavery. "One day, when Moses had grown up, he went out to his people and looked on their burdens; and he saw an Egyptian beating a Hebrew, one of his people". (Ex. 2:11.) It is unlikely that he would have gone "out to his people", concerned himself with "their burdens", worried whether or not any of them was being beaten, if he had not been aware of their plight and of his own identity. Going to see for himself the kind of life they were living and how they were treated suggests that he had set out with

he saw an Egyptian beating a Hebrew ... and ... he killed the Egyptian and hid him in the sand *(Exodus 2:11, 12)*

at least an idea that he might somehow be able to improve their lot — though he could hardly have envisaged that his sight-seeing trip would end in a spontaneous action which would force him to flee the country. He killed the Egyptian overseer who was maltreating the Hebrew serf and buried the body in the sand. Next day, however, trying to stop another fight — this time between two Hebrews — he became alarmed when one of them said "Do you mean to kill me as you killed the Egyptian?" With his action known, it would soon reach the ears of the Pharaoh, and he would be put to death; for attacking, let alone killing, an Egyptian overseer to protect a slave was punishable by execution. Indeed, as the Bible relates, "When Pharaoh heard of it, he sought to kill Moses". Escape was the only course, and he promptly fled eastwards into the Sinai desert.

FUGITIVE IN THE DESERT

Resting at a well, he was helpful to several young maidens who had come to water their father's flocks and were being driven away by shepherds from other tribes. They turned

When Moses killed the Egyptian overseer who was beating a Hebrew slave, he buried his body in the sand, and fled to the wilderness. He was to be reminded of this dramatic episode for the rest of his life for sand dunes were part of the scenery encountered daily by the Israelites during their forty-year sojourn in Sinai.

Now the priest of Midian had seven daughters; and they came and drew water, and filled the troughs to water their father's flock (Exodus 2:16)

Today, as in ancient days, this is how women of the desert (left) carry water from the rare and precious springs to their encampment. For the camels (right) there are troughs, located close to a spring of well. Troughs were common in olden times too, though more primitive.

Moses was keeping the flock of his father-in-law, ...led his flock to the west side of the wilderness, and came to Horeb, the mountain of God (Exodus 3:1)

Shepherds roaming with their flocks (left) in search of scrub and water, as Moses did when he tended the sheep and goats of Jethro, acquiring a familiarity with the desert through which he would later lead his people to freedom. Tents made of goats' hair (right). Throughout the centuries, the tribes of the desert have fashioned their mobile dwellings from materials close at hand.

out to be the daughters of Jethro (also called Reuel), a Midianite priest. (Nomadic clans from the land of Midian, the territory south and southeast of Aqaba, used to wander far afield, and they were a familiar sight in the Sinai peninsula.) When the girls returned to their father, bubbling with their report of the kind "Egyptian" they had met, he told them to invite him to their encampment. Moses came, lived with them and eventually married Jethro's daughter, Zipporah.

Though catapulted so abruptly from royal luxury to primitive life with this Bedouin family, he seems to have adapted well. It was a life of simplicity, looking after his father-in-law's flocks, roaming with them over the desert in search of occasional scrub, watering them, at times sleeping under the heavens, at times returning to the encampment at night, chatting with the wise old Jethro and the other men of the clan round the camp fire, listening to their legends and the stories of their lives and wanderings, absorbing the lore of the desert. From their tales, and from his own day-to-day experiences in the wilderness, he became a "man of the desert", with an

And the angel of the Lord appeared to him in a flame of fire out of the midst of a bush; and he looked, and lo, the bush was burning, yet it was not consumed (Exodus 3:2)

Moses hears of his role of destiny from the divine voice calling to him from the burning bush.
A Byzantine representation (left) in the Monastery of St. Catherine in Sinai; and an illustration in the Golden Haggadah (right), produced in Spain in the early 14th century.

intimate knowledge of the terrain, alive to its manifold dangers, alert to what meager blessings it offered, familiar with its moods in each season. Like the knowledge he had acquired as a prince at the court of the emperor, this knowledge, too, would prove invaluable to him in later years.

Life in the desert gave him something else, perhaps of more profound significance. For the first time, he was in continuous touch with nature, on occasion grim and bleak, on occasion grand and wondrous. He was awed by the blood-red sky at dawn, the star-studded cover of night; by the gaunt face of a primeval crag, by the vast emptiness, the seemingly endless stretch of burning sand, and then the sudden miracle of water. This was all new to Moses, and it was a strange experience. The accustomed Bedouin could accept the familiar. Moses could only wonder — and think. And he thought much as he wandered, alone with his flocks, day after day across the expanse of Sinai. The elements were powerful and mysterious, and clearly wielded by a guiding hand, the hand of that invisible God of whom his sister Miriam had spoken. Surrounded,

as a prince, by temple priests and worship of Egyptian deities, he had found it hard to grasp the extraordinary notion of an all-powerful divinity who could neither be touched nor seen. Now, after years of silent, lonely communion with the phenomena of creation, he could comprehend in full measure the strange concept which had eluded him in his polytheistic youth.

THE REVELATION

It was in this mood that, grazing his flocks near Mount Horeb (Mount Sinai) one day, he chanced upon a burning bush, startled because it was not consumed, and startled even more when out of its flames came the voice of God, the God of Abraham, of Isaac and of Jacob, the names of his forbears which had been whispered to him by Miriam at their secret palace meetings. "Moses, Moses", cried the voice, and he replied "Here am I". Then came the words from out of the fiery bush: "Put off your shoes from your feet, for the place on which you are standing is holy ground". (Ex. 3:5.)

God then told Moses that he had "seen the

40

affliction of my people who are in Egypt" and would "deliver them out of the hand of the Egyptians" and bring them to the Promised Land in fulfilment of his covenant with the Patriarchs. Moses was to be the instrument of their redemption.

In a flash, everything fell into place in Moses' mind. The random events in his past, on which his thoughts had dwelt day and night throughout his years of desert sojourn with Jethro, were like scattered coloured stones which the revelation at Mount Horeb had fashioned into a mosaic with a set design. His rescue from the Nile as a babe, his royal upbringing, the talks with his sister Miriam — and perhaps with other members of the family — the sight of his enslaved people, the killing of the Egyptian overseer, his escape, his years in the wilderness — all suddenly made sense. Each episode had had its purpose, and the overall purpose had been revealed by the divine voice from the flaming bush. His entire life up to this moment had been a preparation for his role of destiny.

And he was ready for it, though he showed an initial reluctance, reciting his deficiencies — perhaps seeking reassurance — and pleading that he was not the right man. God brushed aside his misgivings. He was slow of speech? His brother Aaron, of eloquent tongue, would be his spokesman. He feared the people would not accept his leadership nor believe in his divine mission? God gave him "signs", turning Moses' rod into a serpent and back again into a rod; making his hand leprous and instantly curing it. Using the rod, Moses would "do the signs" (Ex. 4:17) when he reached Egypt.

The words of God ceased. The desert was silent. Moses stood awhile filled with awe, pondering on the mightiness and complexity of the task that lay before him. He had been given the goal — the salvation of his people. Henceforth, without doubt or hesitation, guided by the God of his fathers, he would move inexorably towards it.

The landscape in the new
life of the young Moses,
where he held lonely
communion with the
phenomena of creation.

43

2. THE GREAT FREEDOM TREK

Turning slowly homewards, driving his flock back to his father-in-law's encampment, Moses had time to sort out in his mind the immediate practical steps that had to be taken. He would need to tell Jethro that he was leaving. It would be a wrench for both of them, but he was confident that his father-in-law would understand, and help him with arrangements for the journey. He had wondered whether his mission might not be doomed at the outset with his arrest, as a "wanted" man, the moment he set foot inside Egypt; but God had assured him that by now "all the men who were seeking your life are dead". (Ex. 4:19.) He would need to rouse his own people, straighten their backs, organise them into a compact group, rally them with the cry of freedom, and infuse them with such faith in this dangerous but divine venture that they would break their shackles and follow him out of Egypt. He may well have thought that this might prove immensely more difficult than gaining access to the Pharaoh and moving him to liberate the slaves. For

how indeed could he even begin talking to the Hebrews? If the Egyptian authorities had forgotten him, his people would have forgotten him too, and if he suddenly appeared in their midst, dressed in his desert clothes, and told them what he had come about, they would ridicule him as a sun-crazed Bedouin nomad, more to be pitied than heeded.

THE TWO BROTHERS

On this, however, Moses may have felt reassured, for there is room for speculation that through trusted emissaries from Jethro's clan, word may have been sent to Moses' family that he was alive and well, and periodic contact would have been maintained. The Bible records that God had told Moses: "Aaron, your brother, the Levite....is coming out to meet you", and later, when Moses was on his way, "The Lord said to Aaron, 'Go into the wilderness to meet Moses'." (Ex. 4:27.) Aaron would thus accompany Moses back to Egypt and introduce him to their people. Since he was clearly a distinguished

A dismal field in the land of Goshen.
As State slaves, the Israelite tribes could
work their land only sporadically,
during the brief intervals between
long spells of forced labour.

Foreign chieftains
bringing tribute to the
Egyptian ruler. Wall
painting in a
15th century BC
tomb in Thebes,
the ancient capital
of Upper Egypt.

47

ΟΠΡΟΦΗΤΗϹ
ΖΑΡΡΩΝ
ΠΡΟΦΗΤΗϹ
ΑΑΡΩΝ

The Lord said to Aaron, 'Go into the wilderness to meet Moses.' So he went, and met him at the mountain of God and kissed him (Exodus 4:27)

The brothers Moses and Aaron.
From a painting on wood in
the Byzantine Monastery of
St. Catherine in southern Sinai.

Levite, respected by the Hebrew community of Egypt, his sponsorship would guarantee Moses a sober hearing.

By the time Moses reached home with his flock, his course was clear. He took Jethro aside and told him of his intention to return to Egypt. It is unlikely that he related all that he had experienced at the burning bush, limiting himself to: "Let me go back, I pray, to my kinsmen in Egypt and see whether they are still alive". Jethro replied: "Go in peace." (Ex. 4:18.) So Moses took leave of his father-in-law and the clan, set his wife, Zipporah, and his two sons, Gershom and Eliezer, upon an ass, and they made their way towards Egypt. The rendezvous with Aaron took place en route.

This meeting of the two brothers must have been charged with emotion. But for Moses, it was also a business meeting of great moment. For Aaron would be his principal lieutenant throughout all the imminent struggles, and his initial task would be to pave the way for the community's acceptance of Moses. He had therefore to receive a thorough briefing, and so "Moses told Aaron all the

Moses and Aaron went to Pharaoh and said, 'Thus says the Lord, the God of Israel, Let my people go...'

(Exodus 5:1)

Moses and Aaron in audience
with the Pharaoh (left),
demanding "Let my people go."
In the first plague visited upon
the Egyptians, the waters
of the Nile were turned to
blood (right). Illustrations
in the 14th century
Golden Haggadah from Spain.

51

the locusts came up over all the land of Egypt... they a

'l the plants in the land and all the fruit of the trees

(Exodus 10:14, 15)

Close-up of voracious locusts.
A swarm of locusts descending upon a
field of ripe corn can devour it in
minutes. In the eighth plague,
these insects were so numerous that
they darkened the skies
and settled on every plant.

words of the Lord with which he had sent him, and all the signs which he had charged him to do". (Ex. 4:28.) The two men must also have decided at this wayside desert meeting that the first step would be to meet representatives of the Hebrew community and only then to tackle the Egyptian authorities.

THE TRIBAL PATTERN

The Bible does not elaborate on the pattern of Hebrew society in Egypt at that time, but it is evident that there was a basic organisational framework to the community — the clan and the tribe — within which the brothers could work. Moreover, the people were not scattered. They all lived in and around the Land of Goshen, descendants of the first settlers of this region, Jacob and his sons, the founders of the tribes of Israel, and they belonged to one or another of these tribes. It is also likely that though the community was in bondage, and the official status of each individual was therefore that of a State slave, they were not necessarily engaged in slave labour at all times. What it meant was that the authorities could call upon the community

The Exodus of the Israelites from Egypt was so hasty
that they had to take "their dough before it was leavened."
This is commemorated during the Jewish Festival of
Passover by the eating of **matza,** unleavened bread.
There are parts of Sinai where **matza** is still baked in
the ancient way, as shown in these photographs.
The dough (flour and water) is being kneaded (above),
a pit prepared and glowing charcoal placed at the bottom.
The rolled dough is spread over the charcoal, covered by
another layer of charcoal (below), and left to bake.
The thin **matza** (right) is removed from the pit.

.it was not leavened, because they… could not tarry…
(Exodus 12:39)

This month [Nissan] shall be for you the beginning of months *(Exodus 12:2)*

The spring season, headed by the Hebrew month of Nissan, represented in the lower half of this detail in the well-preserved mosaic of the Zodiac circle discovered in the early 4th century synagogues of Hamat-Tiberias on the Sea of Galilee. Nissan, the month of the Festival of Passover, appears in Hebrew lettering, bottom left.

at any time to provide labourers without pay for whatever tasks they desired. Whether they would take all the males in the community or only some, whether for a long or a short period, whether for tough physical labour or light duties, whether with prior warning or with none, would depend on the whim of the Pharaoh and whether he was well or ill disposed towards the Hebrews. During the reign of a less harsh ruler, the Israelites would have more time at home, cultivating their fields and grazing their flocks. When they were taken off on forced labour, their families would have to manage as best they could.

But whatever the system, all were members of one or another of the twelve Hebrew tribal groups, and they would look to their tribal leaders for guidance on their communal affairs. It was thus natural for Moses and Aaron to operate through these leaders, who would no doubt consult with the heads of their clans in the formulation and implementation of tribal policy. For Moses to secure the trust and support of his people, the obvious first step was to gain acceptance by these elders of the community. Their endorsement would

...with unleavened bread and bitter herbs they shall eat it. ...It is the Lord's passover *(Exodus 12:8, 11)*

The Seder service on the first night of Passover is celebrated in Jewish homes throughout the world. All recite the story of the Exodus, say the same prayers, serve the same symbolic dishes. This family, conducting the Seder in Jerusalem, came from Yemen.

ensure popular backing for Moses' mission of rescue. And so "Moses and Aaron went and gathered together all the elders of the people of Israel", and at this crucial first meeting, upon which so much hung, "Aaron spoke all the words which the Lord had spoken to Moses, and did the signs in the sight of the people". (Ex. 4:29, 30.)

Behind these brief and bare biblical phrases lies the drama of what must have transpired at this first encounter. Aaron, with Moses at his side, sought to arouse the tribal leaders with the revolutionary appeal to create a resistance movement. Their plight, as they well knew, was insufferable, their freedom lost and the bulk of their people in bondage. Worse, they had been without hope, passively accepting their misfortune as a natural disaster, holding it, no doubt, to have been decreed from on high. Well, Aaron told them, he had come to announce the stupendous news that their days of slavery were coming to an end. God had told Moses that he had not forgotten his people, nor his promise to their forefathers, the Patriarchs. He was aware of their sufferings, had seen their affliction and had resolved

Samaritan Passover scene on Mount
Gerizim. The Samaritans are an ancient
sect who were brought to Samaria by
the Assyrians after their conquest of the
northern Kingdom of Israel in the
8th century BC, and who later adopted
a form of Judaism, in which the Five
Books of Moses (the Torah) alone were
accepted as sacred scripture, and Mount
Gerizim in Samaria was considered holy.
It is on this mountain that they
assemble on Passover, sacrifice the
paschal lamb and eat it in haste, as is
written in the Torah.

to launch them into freedom. The moment of salvation had arrived.

It is probable that despite Aaron's eloquence and the towering presence of the brooding Moses, the tribal leaders were sceptical. It was all very well for Aaron to say that God had spoken to Moses — but had he also spoken to Pharaoh? In the grim practical day-to-day world in which they lived, were they expected calmly to tell their Egyptian task-masters that they no longer felt themselves slaves and would not be reporting for work in the morning? The ring-leaders would be executed and the rest would be beaten and shackled. What good would it do them to claim that they were acting in accordance with the will of God? Who would believe them? And even if they were believed, of what account was "their God" to the Egyptian overseers? Come to think of it, why should they, the tribal leaders, believe Aaron?

It was presumably at that point that Aaron "did the signs", performing the miracles that had been displayed to Moses in the desert. And this must have reassured the leaders. They were convinced, and ready now to hear what initial steps Moses and Aaron proposed to take.

It was then that the two brothers outlined their course of action. It meant nothing less than a general uprising, the conversion of the entire Israelite community into a resistance movement. Its object would not be to overthrow the existing pharaonic regime — that was both beyond their scope and capability, and also unnecessary; for the aim was not to make Egypt a land in which the Hebrews might continue to live without suffering. The purpose was to take them out of Egypt and bring them to their own promised land where they could create and be masters of their own religious and national life.

Neither Aaron nor Moses was disposed to minimise the extreme difficulties and dangers that lay ahead. They would not, in the first instance, call upon the slaves to turn on their masters. The might of Egypt was such that the rebellion would be crushed quickly, and if the slaves were thought to be more trouble than they were worth, there would be no compunction about slaughtering them. No. What needed to be done was to effect a change

The stained glass
windows of Marc
Chagall in the synagogue
at the Hadassah-
Hebrew University
Medical Centre in
Jerusalem. Each window-
painting depicts the
characteristics
of one of the twelve
tribes of Israel,
as described
in the Bible.

63

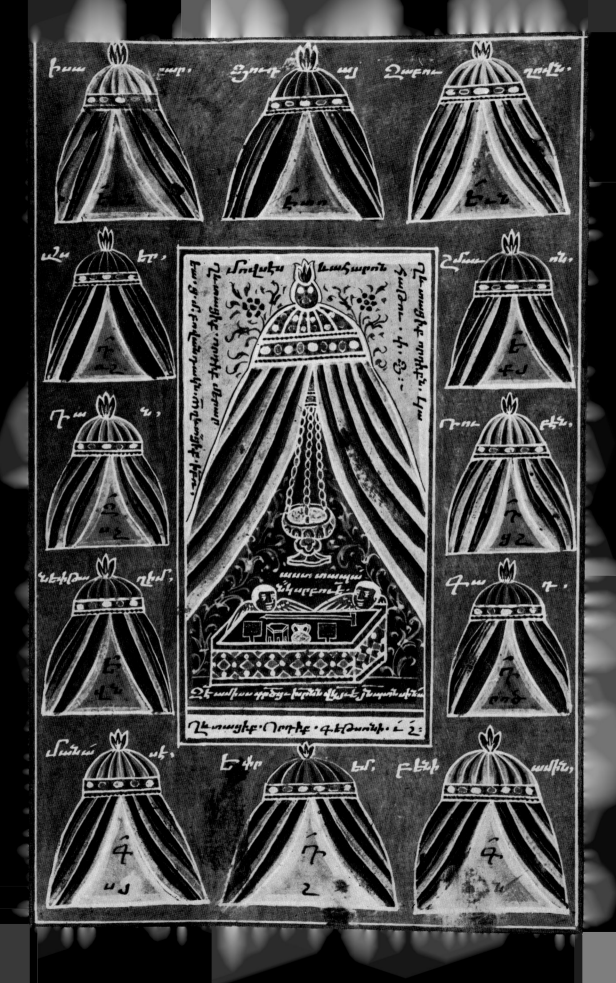

The twelves tribes, represented by tents,
grouped round the Tabernacle
containing the Ark of the Covenant.
From a 17th century illuminated
manuscript in the Library of St. Thoros,
attached to the Armenian Orthodox
Patriarchate, Jerusalem.

of heart in the Pharaoh. He had to be per-
suaded to free the Hebrew slaves and allow
them to leave the country. That was the func-
tion which Moses, with Aaron as his aide,
would take upon himself, guided in all his
actions by the Lord.

The leaders responded to this call, but they
were evidently doubtful whether they could
convince their people, and they must have
asked Aaron and Moses to repeat their "signs"
at a mass gathering. What had impressed
them would assuredly impress the public, and
so after this initial vital meeting with the tribal
chiefs, the Bible says that Aaron "did the
signs in the sight of the people". The response
was instant and unanimous. "And the people
believed; and when they heard that the Lord
had visited the people of Israel and that he
had seen their affliction, they bowed their
heads and worshipped." (Ex. 4:31.)

A FATEFUL MEETING

Armed with the support of the community,
Moses and Aaron could now take their next
decisive step: the approach to the Pharaoh.
The first hurdle was the technical problem of
securing an audience with the ruler. There are
several theories as to how this was effected.
Some scholars have suggested that an appropriate word was whispered in the royal ear
by one of the former court companions of
Moses, or one of the surviving palace officials
who had known Moses as a boy. It is also
possible that Moses' foster-mother, the princess, may still have been alive and used her
good offices with the king. But perhaps
Moses was able to gain the royal presence by
much simpler means. A contemporary scribe
wrote of the delights of living in the restored
town of Avaris, the ancient Hyksos capital
which Rameses II had reconstructed with the
labour of the Hebrew slaves and re-named
Raamses. In the course of his account, the
scribe wrote: "Oh, the joy of dwelling there....
No wish is unfulfilled: the humble man and
the mighty are as one...all men equally can
lay their requests before him [Pharaoh]."
Apparently, unlike other, less approachable,
rulers, Rameses II introduced the custom of
holding an occasional "open house" to which
any member of the public could come with a
plea or a complaint. The suggestion, there-

The thermal spring of Hamam
Far'aoun on the east bank of the
Gulf of Suez and the western
edge of the Sinai desert.
The name is Arabic for the
"hot waters of Pharaoh".
According to local legend this is
where the Egyptian chariots
pursuing the Israelites were
bogged, and Pharaoh's anger
and alarm raised the temperature
of the waters.

The Sinai Peninsula photographed from
American space-ship Gemini 8. Sinai is
the triangle in the middle of the
photograph, bounded by the Gulf of Suez
on the left and the Gulf of Eilat on the right.

fore, is that all Moses had to do was appear
at the palace on one such occasion and join
the line of supplicants waiting to be admitted
to the throne room.

However the audience was arranged, the
moment arrived when Moses and Aaron
found themselves face to face with Pharaoh.
Though the biblical record of this meeting is
brief, it is evident that the two Hebrews
showed no sense of awe in the presence of
the mighty Egyptian ruler. They did not come
to beg, cap in hand, nor grovel at the master's
feet. Armed with the guidance of the all-
powerful Lord, they entered with heads erect
and spoke with confidence. But at this first
meeting, they did not raise the vital issue of
liberating the enslaved Hebrews. As a tactical
opening, they simply sought the Pharaoh's
permission to allow them to pray and sacrifice to their God at a place "three days'
journey into the wilderness". "Thus says the
Lord, the God of Israel", they said to the
ruler. "Let my people go, that they may hold
a feast to me in the wilderness." (Ex. 5:1.)

The king's response was predictable. He
was outraged. For one thing, he was not
accustomed to the posture of confidence,
almost that of equal-to-equal, among his
menial supplicants. For another, it was un-
heard of for slaves to be given an extended
holiday. To grant them such a right would set
a dangerous precedent, prompting similar
demands for privileges from other slave
groups, and where would it all end? It might
upset the entire Egyptian social system. And
what a preposterous excuse for taking leave
from their labours: to worship "their God"
in the wilderness! "Who is the Lord, that
I should heed his voice and let Israel go?"
(Ex. 5:2.)

THE CALL TO RESISTANCE

As soon as Moses and Aaron were dismissed,
the Pharaoh gave instructions that the work
load of the Hebrew slaves be increased. Their
daily quota of brick-making was to remain,
but now, instead of being provided with straw
they would have to scurry around and gather
their own straw. This would teach them to
remember who they were, and what to expect
if they were ever again moved to be so pre-
sumptuous. It would also, as he shrewdly

68

The Egyptians pursued them, all Pharaoh's ... chario

Pharaoh's chariot. Detail from a
14th century BC painting on the
side panel of a wooden chest
discovered in the tomb of
Tutankhamun at Thebes.

...nd his horsemen... overtook them... at the sea *(Exodus 14:9)*

the people of Israel went into the midst of the sea on dry
hand over the sea…' The waters returned and covered the

*round... Then the Lord said to Moses, 'Stretch out your
...ariots and all the host of Pharaoh (Exodus 14:22, 26, 28)*

Two pictures from a 1601 Armenian
illuminated Hymnal in the Library
of St. Thoros, Jerusalem, illustrating,
on the right, the Children of Israel
reaching dry land after the waters had
parted, and, on the left, the luckless
Egyptian troops caught by the
returning seas. The artist has linked
the two scenes with the staff of Moses.

anticipated, set the slaves against their leaders.

He was right. Their anger over their added burdens was directed less at their Egyptian task-masters than at Moses. He had come to them with magic words and the promise of freedom, and here they were with "heavier work" laid upon them and subjected to further beatings. "The Lord look upon you and judge", they said to Moses, "because you have made us offensive in the sight of Pharaoh and his servants, and have put a sword in their hand to kill us." (Ex. 5:21.)

Thus was one of the first major resistance movements in history faced with a key problem which would be encountered by every subsequent movement to resist oppression, right down to our own day: how to stir the masses to rise above their fear of reprisals, that fear which keeps them passive. It is no light matter — and it certainly was not in the Egypt of those days — for the weak and unarmed to defy authority; but a few sturdy souls, setting the example which releases the pent-up feelings of a downtrodden community, can launch a successful revolt.

Moses understood this, and he knew, following the Pharaoh's punitive action, that he needed to instil in his people the will to resist. This could never have been an easy task, and it was more difficult for Moses since he had to deal with a loosely organised community, lacking cohesion, their senses dulled and their spirits dampened by years of enslavement. He resolved, therefore, to seek out the leading men of the tribes and clans and he held countless meetings with them, trying to quicken their spirit, change their outlook, give them ideals and new horizons, and, without minimizing the dangers and the casualties they would suffer in the long struggle ahead, inject them with hope and with confidence in their capacities. He was able to win them over — as he had earlier won their acceptance of him as leader — through their faith in God, the God of their Patriarchs. He had abandoned them, but he had now remembered them; and there was a persuasive conviction behind Moses' words because he himself believed so profoundly in God and in the fulfilment of God's promise. Not all revolts are successful, and not every

An area near the northern end of Suez which is left marshy when the waters recede. A minority theory on the route of the Exodus holds that this is where the Egyptian chariots got stuck, and were engulfed when the waters returned.

resistance leader is free of doubt. But Moses, moved by the spirit of God, at no time doubted that the mission of liberation would succeed.

Armed with this support from the elders, Moses could now proceed to the next phase of his resistance campaign. He recognised that no Egyptian ruler would free his slaves upon request. No man of power ever relinquishes power willingly. He does so only when he is compelled to, either by armed force or by the creation of circumstances which turn the tenure of power into a liability (like the reluctant grant of independance to subject peoples in our own generation).

Moses commanded no armed force. Other means would be required to induce Pharaoh to "let my people go". God provided them by causing the ten plagues to descend upon the land of Egypt. As each became insufferable, Pharaoh agreed to let the Israelites leave; but as each affliction was lifted, he changed his mind. "I will harden Pharaoh's heart", said the Lord, reassuring Moses who would otherwise have been dismayed at Pharaoh's successive betrayals. But the moun-

ting impact as plague followed plague would prove so shattering that the ruler would wish to see the last of the Hebrew slaves.

First, the waters of the Nile were turned to blood. Then came the plague of frogs. Then gnats, attacking man and beast. Then swarms of flies in every home throughout Egypt — except in Goshen where the Israelites dwelt. This was followed by a plague on Egyptian cattle — but not on "the cattle of Israel". Then came an epidemic of boils; a devastating hailstorm; clouds of voracious locusts; and a three-day spell of utter darkness.

These natural disasters, divinely decreed, were not chosen at random. They were designed to strike at Pharaoh at the very centre of his power. The celebrated Egyptologist Professor Pierre Montet has pointed out — in connection with the heavy pharaonic preoccupation with the building of temples and monuments to the gods and goddesses of Egypt — that each Pharaoh believed and wished his people to believe that he was divine and divinely chosen. This was the condition of his authority. "Provided that the gods appointed as sovereign... the issue of their

divine flesh, then the land would enjoy peace and prosperity. A swelling Nile would cover the earth with wheat and barley, flocks would multiply... But all depended on the fulfilment of this basic condition. If that were not satisfied, the land of Egypt would drift aimlessly; none would wield authority, for all would be striving to command. Brother would slay brother... Then no longer would the Nile flood the land. Starvation would stalk the earth. No imports would enter... no offerings be presented in the temples to the gods, who would in consequence avert their eyes from those who had deserted their faith. Thus the Pharaoh's prime duty was to demonstrate his gratitude to the divine rulers of the universe...."

The plagues which now afflicted the land, polluting the Nile, destroying the crops, killing the flocks, bringing starvation and misery, were the catastrophes most likely to call into question the divine choice of the Pharaoh. And it was this more than anything else — more than a concern for his people's sufferings — that was calculated to move the Pharaoh towards the unprecedented step of

freeing one of his slave communities; for it endangered the foundations of his authority.

THE FIRST PASSOVER

The final calamity, however, the tenth and grimmest of all, inflicted deep personal suffering on the Pharaoh too. This was the death of the first-born in every Egyptian family, high and low. It was timed for the night of the fourteenth of the Hebrew month of Nissan, and the Lord told Moses and Aaron to prepare the Israelites for that night — and for their immediate exodus from the land of Egypt.

Four days before, every Israelite family was to bring home a lamb or a kid. On the evening of the fourteenth, it was to be slaughtered, and some of its blood daubed on the doorposts and lintel of each house. This sign would mark off the Hebrew homes which would be passed over when the Lord came to smite the Egyptians. The flesh of the animal should be roasted and eaten that night in this manner: "your loins girded, your sandals on your feet, and your staff in your hand; and you shall eat it in haste. It is the Lord's passover." (Ex. 12:11) At midnight, the Lord struck, and the first-born of all the Egyptians died. A great cry went up in the land, and that night the Pharaoh summoned Moses and Aaron and urged them to "Rise up, go forth from among my people, both you and the people of Israel; and go, serve the Lord, as you have said. Take your flocks and your herds... and be gone; and bless me also!" (Ex. 12:31, 32.) The Egyptian people also urged the Hebrews to hurry out, and gave them jewels and other valuables to speed their departure. They promptly left, setting out in a southeasterly direction for Sinai. They had taken their first step along the road to freedom.

God had told Moses: "This day shall be for you a memorial day... throughout your generations you shall observe it as an ordinance for ever." (Ex. 12:14.) To this day, Jews throughout the world celebrate the seven-day spring festival of Passover to commemorate the Exodus. It is the great Jewish festival of freedom. On the first night, there is a ritual meal, called the Seder, in which all members of the family participate. They read the Haggada, which recounts the story of the Exodus, and partake of special foods symbolic of the dramatic events of that liberation. They eat *matza*, unleavened bread, to remind them of the hasty departure of their forebears. ("So the people took their dough before it was leavened". [Ex. 12:34].) They taste bitter herbs to recall the harsh life and labours of the Israelites in Egypt. And they place a shank bone on the table to represent the paschal lamb whose blood was sprinkled on the Israelite dwellings on that fateful night. Four goblets of ritual wine are drunk during the recital of the Exodus story. Perhaps the most impressive passage in the Haggada is the one which points to the key purpose of the Passover festival—the occasion when every Jew can feel a personal identification with these happenings in his people's past, as if he himself were an Israelite launching himself into freedom: "Each individual in every generation should look upon himself as though he personally had gone forth from Egypt. As it is said: 'And thou shalt tell thy son on this day: This is on account of what

The lush oasis of Kadesh Barnea,
which the Israelites were not to
reach for another two years.

the Lord did for me when I came out of
Egypt.' Not only our forefathers did the Holy
One redeem, but us, too, did he redeem with
them."

EXODUS

Clan by clan and tribe by tribe, the Hebrews
with their flocks began their great trek. Their
first stop was Succoth, just west of today's
Ismailia, and from there they proceeded to
Etham, "on the edge of the wilderness"; and
"the Lord went before them by day in a
pillar of cloud to lead them along the way,
and by night in a pillar of fire to give them
light". (Ex. 13:21.) They then moved off
towards the Reed Sea and encamped on its
western shore. (The "Red Sea" [Ex. 13:18] is
the incorrect English translation of the Hebrew *Yam-Suf,* which means, literally, "Sea
of Reeds". We shall be considering its probable location later.) Here, at the water's edge,
they were to suffer their first traumatic
experience — and enjoy one of their greatest
triumphs.

It took several days for the Egyptians to
start recovering from the series of severe

blows which had suddenly smitten them. The first-born had been buried, the Nile was no longer red, the air was free of gnats and flies, and life was beginning to return to normal. One feature alone was missing from the Egyptian scene: the Israelite slaves. Pharaoh and his advisers, no longer under the pressure of catastrophe, pondered the events of the previous weeks, climaxed by the flight of the Hebrews. And they were incensed. Had they been tricked? Could the "God" of whom Moses and Aaron had spoken really have been responsible for the plagues? Most of them, after all, were disasters with which Egypt was familiar from time to time, though assuredly the country had never experienced them all at once. The more they thought about it, the stronger became their conviction that they had been victims of a gigantic hoax; and now, in addition to all they had suffered in the plagues, they had lost a sizeable element of their slave labour force. This was a significant loss in itself. More important, it could have a grave impact on the other forced-labour units, who might equally take it into their heads to rebel and leave. Immediate action

was called for, and the Pharaoh accordingly "made ready his chariot", mobilized his army, "and took six hundred picked chariots and all the other chariots of Egypt with officers over all of them" (Ex. 14:7) and set off in pursuit of the Hebrews. Though he was starting out several days later, the king with his mobile squadrons would soon overtake his slow-moving former bondsmen. He caught up with them at the edge of the Reed Sea.

The Israelites saw them approaching, and Moses faced his first major crisis of leadership. His people were seized with fear. There they were, an unarmed group of men, women and children, sprawled out with their flocks at the edge of the sea, watching a huge and disciplined body of angry Egyptian charioteers riding down upon them. Hemmed in by the water, there was no escape, and in their terror, they turned upon Moses. Their impending slaughter was all due to his high-flown talk of liberation. Why had he brought them out of Egypt? Why could he not have left them there? True, they would have been slaves, but at least they would have been alive. Now they faced slaughter. "Is it because there are no

When Pharaoh let the people go, God did not lead them by way of the land of the Philistines, although that was near (Exodus 13:17)

The "Way of the Sea" was the coastal
highway linking Egypt with Damascus
used by commercial caravans
and imperial armies. According to
one theory, the Israelites left Egypt
by this route before turning south into
the desert. Remains of ancient fortifications
which guarded this highway.

The oasis of Wadi Firan today, believed to be the site of biblical Elim, well-watered and thick with palm and tamarisk, which refreshed the spirits of the Israelites after their disappointment at Marah.

82

graves in Egypt that you have taken us away to die in the wilderness?" (Ex. 14:11.) The biblical record then provides the hint that Moses had not found it easy to rouse the populace to rise up against their task-masters and follow him. For they cried: "Is not this what we said to you in Egypt, 'Let us alone and let us serve the Egyptians'?" (Ex. 14:12.) As at every critical turn in the fortunes of any resistance movement, there would be a good deal of grumbling and murmuring and down-right rebellion on the part of the doubters and the weak in faith before the great freedom trek was over.

THE WATERS PART

Guided by the Lord, Moses had now to exert all his powers of leadership and decisiveness of action to save the day. He must have displayed supreme confidence, stilling their anxieties and infecting them with his own unwavering faith in their destiny. "Fear not", he told his people, "stand firm, and see the salvation of the Lord". (Ex. 14:13.) Night fell; the Egyptian force halted, ready to do battle in the morning; and Moses ordered the

Israelites to get ready for a speedy departure. At day-break, "Moses stretched out his hand over the sea; and the Lord drove the sea back by a strong east wind all night, and made the sea dry land, and the waters were divided." (Ex. 14:21.) The Israelites promptly set out across this dry ground — for even the hesitant felt they had nothing to lose. To have remained behind would have put them at the mercy of the Egyptian army.

Shortly afterwards, the pursuing forces appeared on the scene. Noting that the waters had given way to dry land, which was firm enough to hold the fleeing Israelites, they immediately followed. But the ground which was hard enough to walk across proved too soft to resist the inroads of a chariot force, and it "discomfited the host of the Egyptians, clogging their chariot wheels so that they drove heavily". (Ex. 14:24, 25.) Horses and vehicles got bogged in the mud and stuck, and before they could turn back, "The waters returned and covered the chariots and the horsemen and all the host of Pharaoh that had followed them into the sea". (Ex. 14:28.) All were drowned. The Israelites were saved.

The remains of ancient fortifications in Wadi Firan, then as now one of the principal oases in southwestern Sinai.

Where did this encounter take place? There are various theories as to the location of the Reed Sea, each tied to a particular theory of the overall route of the Exodus. These broadly fall into two categories, some scholars holding to a northern route, others to a southern route. There is much to be said for both, and each can draw on biblical references and modern archaeological discoveries for support; but most modern scholars tend largely towards the southern route.

According to the "northern" scholars, the Reed Sea was what is now known as the Bardawil Lake, lying between Kantara and El Arish from west to east, and, from north to south, between the Mediterranean and the sand dunes of northern Sinai. It is separated from the Mediterranean by a very narrow strip of land, ranging in width from 100 yards to half a mile. This strip formed part of the great coastal highway from Egypt to Canaan and Mesopotamia in ancient times, called in the Bible the "way of the land of the Philistines". The waters of Bardawil are extremely shallow (barely a foot and a half in parts) even today when, at various points along the

they moved on from Succoth, and encamped at Etham

(Exodus 13:20)

"I made the people of Israel dwell in booths when I brought them out of the land of Egypt". (Lev. 23:43) The booths of a tribal settlement in northeastern Sinai today.

strip, great chunks have been excavated to enable the waters of the Mediterranean to flow into the lake (and so enrich its stock of fish). In ancient times, when the strip was intact, it must have been much shallower. Moreover, this lake is swept by uncommonly strong winds, and at times the shallowest parts are barely covered by water. It is therefore suggested that an Israelite crossing of Bardawil from the narrow northern strip southwards to the sand dunes would match the biblical account. The Egyptian chariots, coming after them, would have got stuck in the bed of the lake and then, with the wind changing in intensity or direction, the waters would have risen and engulfed them.

From here, according to this theory, the remaining route through the wilderness would have been confined to the northern stretch of the Sinai peninsula. Where, then, would the scholars place Mount Sinai? None can commit himself to a specific location, but some have suggested Jebel Hilel as the possible site. It is a mountain in northeastern Sinai lying to the southwest of Abu Ageila and Jebel Libne, names made famous in our

The gnarled trunk of an ancient tree in Wadi Firan, the oasis through which the Israelites passed on their way to Mount Sinai.

own day in the Sinai battles of 1956 and 1967. From here, the Israelites would have continued a short distance eastwards to Kadesh Barnea, where they remained for most of their wilderness years. If scholars differ over the location of the Reed Sea and Mount Sinai, all are agreed — even those who subscribe to the "southern-route" theory — that Kadesh Barnea is the large oasis in northeastern Sinai now known as Ain el-Kudeirat, near Kusseima, some 50 miles south of Beersheba.

The "southern" theory — that the Israelites reached Kadesh Barnea only after wandering round southern Sinai — would appear to fit the biblical account more smoothly. It is also based on an ancient tradition. Moreover, the Bible says: "When Pharaoh let the people go, God did not lead them by way of the land of the Philistines [the northern coastal highway], although that was near; for God said, 'Lest the people repent when they see war, and return to Egypt'." (Ex. 13:17.) They would certainly have seen a good deal of war had they taken — and kept to — the northern highway along the Mediterranean coast. For precisely because it "was near" and the

direct route, it was heavily used by armies and trading caravans, the last people runaway slaves would have wished to encounter. The "northern" theorists are well aware of this apparent contradiction, but claim that Moses only started out along the northern road, but then crossed southwards over Lake Bardawil. This would have brought him to the area of the dunes, which was untravelled in those days.

However, the "southern" theorists hold that the Israelites turned to the southeast soon after leaving Egypt, and they identify the Reed Sea with the Bitter Lakes, which lie between today's Ismailia and Suez, the port at the northern end of the Gulf of Suez. The Great Bitter Lake is divided from the Little Bitter Lake by straits where the water is shallow even today. But before the construction of the Suez Canal, it was not an uncommon feature for the straits to become dry, exposing a narrow strand which one could easily walk across. This occurred at times when the water level fell in the Gulf of Suez. When it rose again, the water would begin to seep through the bed of the straits, turning

Jebel Mussa, the "Mount of Moses", in the heart of the gaunt and rugged range that towers above the southern region of the peninsula and marks it off from the north. An early Christian tradition held this to be the site of Mount Sinai where Moses received the Ten Commandments.

it into mud, and a little while later, there would be a sudden flood, the water rushing through, covering the straits and obliterating the division between the two Bitter Lakes. It must be said that this phenomenon matches perfectly the biblical report. It explains the fear of the Israelites encamped at the edge of the strand — without knowing it — when the water was high, seeing no escape from the advancing Egyptians; the waters "divided" at day-break, with the Great Bitter Lake on one side and the Little Bitter Lake on the other; the Egyptian chariots mired in the mud; and then the waters rushing through to cover them.

According to this "southern" theory, after crossing the Bitter Lakes and moving a little distance inland, the Israelites proceeded due south along the eastern shore of the Gulf of Suez, past today's Port Taufiq, Ras Sudar and Abu Rudeis, and then turned east into Wadi Firan, and on to Mount Sinai. No scholar is prepared to identify Mount Sinai as today's Jebel Mussa, but an early Christian tradition held this gaunt peak in the wild, forbidding and rugged mountain country of the southern Sinai peninsula to have been the mountain where Moses received the Ten Commandments. In the 4th century AD, the emperor Constantine erected a chapel to mark what was believed to be the site of the Burning Bush at the foot of a nearby lower slope, as well as a refuge tower for hermits. In the 6th century, the emperor Justinian I added an entire monastery complex and enclosed the whole with a high wall of grey granite. Several centuries later it became known as St. Catherine's Monastery, and today's structure is basically the fortress-like building of Justinian.

Whatever the exact location of Mount Sinai, the "southern" theorists consider that it was somewhere in the mountainous southern region of the peninsula. By taking this route, the Israelites would have been least likely to encounter Egyptian troops. Nor would they meet them when, after the Giving of the Law, they would have proceeded northeastwards, perhaps along the western shore of today's Gulf of Eilat, and northwards to Kadesh Barnea.

It must be said, however, that in terms of the history of Israel, any discussion of the

Come up to me on the mountain, and wait there

(Exodus 24:12)

Some three thousand steps reach up to the "gateway to heaven", as it is sometimes called, at the summit of Jebel Mussa.

Exodus route is only of academic interest. For the basic fact remains that no matter where in the Sinai peninsula the ceremony took place at which the Commandments and the Covenant were received, it was that momentous occasion which laid the foundations for the Jewish religion and Jewish nationhood.

CRISIS IN SINAI

When the Israelites "saw the Egyptians dead upon the sea shore", they sang a song of thankfulness and glory to the Lord, and Miriam, sister of Moses, took a timbrel in her hand and led the women in dance. Their spirits were high and their confidence in Moses was restored. But three days later, after trekking through the scorching Wilderness of Shur, they came up against the key problem of all travellers in the desert — water. Arriving at Marah, they found its water too bitter to drink — Marah is Hebrew for bitter — "And the people murmured againt Moses". (Ex. 15:24.) This was to be the pattern during the wilderness years, the people reacting to variations in fortune with the predictability of

95

St. Catherine's Monastery, set against the mountains of southern Sinai, located, according to early Christian belief, near the site of the burning bush. Monks and hermits were attracted to this spot.

litmus to acid and alkali. When things went well, they were content, and full of quiet respect for Moses. When things went badly, they were plunged in despair and promptly castigated him. It was understandable. They were not a picked group of educated, trained and dedicated idealists, with a burning passion for freedom, determined to withstand all hardship to achieve their goal. They were a simple people, born bondsmen, brought up without hope, who were suddenly jerked out of their grim but familiar life-pattern and thrust into a strange and dangerous nomadic existence. Moses had come with his magic offer of freedom, accompanied by awesome signs from God, and to them it was conceived as a gift, presented on a miraculous platter. Although Moses must surely have told them that the road would be long and hard, they had been thinking only in the limited terms of their day-to-day experience. Freedom meant immediate relief from rigorous labour and painful beatings. True, it had been gained, and they were now beyond the reach of their Egyptian slave-drivers. But was the wilderness any better, with its heat and cold,

hunger and thirst, and the constant fear of attack by predatory nomad bands? Moses and their tribal leaders had told them that it was — that as bondsmen they had been without land and without a future, whereas now they were on their way to both. But such talk did not fill an empty belly nor moisten a parched throat. They were beginning to realise that what Moses had offered them was not a neatly tied package labelled "freedom" but the opportunity to struggle for it. It would be one of the slowest and most painful tasks of Moses' leadership — but ultimately the most rewarding — to educate his people willingly to fight and suffer for an exalted ideal. When the time came for the conquest and settlement of the promised land, they, or rather their children, would be ready.

But now, at Marah, they were complaining of thirst, and the water was brackish. Why had Moses brought them there? It is reasonable to assume that this was territory with which he was very familiar. He must have recognised every tree, every rock, and certainly every oasis from his years of wandering with Jethro's flocks. Moreover, as an experienced

96

The oasis of Ein Furtaga in eastern Sinai. This is a rare photograph of a "sea in the desert", waters rushing down after heavy rains in the distant north and briefly trapped in a flash-flood in the wadi.

99

Part of a primitive hunting scene (right) with camel riders and trappers on foot, scratched on sandstone rock. Graffiti by travellers and pilgrims of different historical periods are to be found along the caravan routes throughout Sinai. Among the rock drawings found in Sinai was this representation of a menorah (left), the seven-branched candelabrum described in the vision of Zechariah (4:2) which became the Jewish symbol of the light of the spirit and its supremacy over might. The menorah was one of the ritual vessels in the Second Temple. It is today the emblem of the State of Israel.

100

desert shepherd, he would plan the route and halts in his movement orders for the Israelites in accordance with the location of sweet water springs. He should therefore have known that the waters of Marah were undrinkable.

The fact is that even with the most disciplined force and the most meticulous logistic planning, unexpected obstacles confound the time-table. It would have been worse confounded with the straggling tribal groups of Israelites. Flocks strayed, families got sick, the children were tired and could not keep up, and some clan wardens were less effective than others. Since they had to move in a single body for protection, their pace was dictated by the slowest straggler. Moreover, though they would refill their water-skins at each spring, poor water-discipline would exhaust their reserves before they reached the next planned halt. This was a problem Moses had to contend with frequently in the period immediately following the Exodus.

At Marah God told Moses to throw a certain tree into the water which made it drinkable. He then pressed on to Elim, and

We remember the fish we ate in Egypt for nothing
(Numbers 11:5)

A wall painting in a tomb discovered in Thebes belonging to the 13th century BC, the period of the Exodus. It suggests "the fleshpots" of Egypt after which the Israelites hankered when they suffered spells of hunger during their early months in the desert, and railed against Moses.

this, rather than Marah, may well have been the stop he had planned, for at Elim, "there were twelve springs of water and seventy palm trees", and there the tribes encamped. (The probable identification of Elim as today's Oasis of Wadi Firan has been suggested. The mouth of this wadi is just off the east bank of the Gulf of Suez, some 2 miles south of Abu Rudeis, and it winds eastwards into Sinai, climbing between tall granite mountains until it reaches a magnificent oasis, some 2,000 feet above sea level, set amidst lofty peaks. Lush and picturesque, well-watered and thick with palm trees and tamarisks, it is one of the surprises of arid southern Sinai. Even the modern traveller comes upon it with joyous relief after a hot and dusty drive. To the ancient Israelites, it must have been a sight of miraculous wonder.)

The next move was into the "wilderness of Sin" and they soon ran out of food. Again there was grumbling, the people railing against Moses and Aaron for taking them away from "the fleshpots" of Egypt where they "ate bread to the full". (Ex. 16:3.) Moses admonished them for complaining and then

In the evening quails came up and covered the camp

(Exodus 16:13)

The Lord sent them quails. Migrating quails still flock to Sinai, and until recently were caught in nets. Trapping was easy, for the birds were tired after their long flight across the Mediterranean. Israel's Nature Reserve Authority has prohibited this practice.

assured them of the Lord's promise that he would provide "in the evening flesh to eat and in the morning bread to the full". What followed were the miracles of quails and manna. Incidentally, these are still features of Sinai desert life. Migrating flocks of quails come in to rest at night among the desert scrub and until recently were netted in immense quantities. (This is now forbidden.) Manna is described in the Bible as "a fine, flake-like thing, fine as hoarfrost ... like coriander seed, white, and the taste of it was like wafers made with honey". (Ex. 16:14, 31.) Botanists say it calls to mind the resin-like substance that is exuded by the tamarisk trees in Sinai and which drops to the ground.

Pushing deeper into the wilderness by gentle stages, they came to Rephidim and again ran out of water. This time their complaints so exasperated Moses that he cried to the Lord: "What shall I do with this people? They are almost ready to stone me." (Ex. 17:4.) Moses was told to gather the elders together and in their presence strike a rock. He did so and fresh water gushed out. (In the mountainous country of southern Sinai, there is a porous rock which gives forth water when struck.) Moses called the place "Massah and Meribah", Hebrew for "Testing and Contention", because of the "faultfinding of the children of Israel, and because they put the Lord to the proof by saying, 'Is the Lord among us or not'." (This account appears in Exodus 17:1–7 and relates to Rephidim. It is regarded by scholars as more faithful than the similar, though not identical, version in Numbers 20:1–13, which places the action in Kadesh.)

MILITARY ENCOUNTER

It was at Rephidim that the untrained, untried Israelites, with no army organisation, experienced their first military encounter. They were attacked by a band of Amalekites. The name Amalekites is applied throughout the Bible to the large groups of desert nomads who roamed Sinai and the northern areas of the Arabian desert seeking plunder from the trading caravans and occasionally raiding farm settlements near the edge of the wilderness. The slow-trekking Israelites must have seemed to them a tempting target.

Sneaking up on the Israelites when these were "faint and weary", they struck at their rear, taking them by surprise and causing havoc to "all who lagged behind". Moses promptly summoned Joshua the son of Nun, of the tribe of Ephraim, and ordered him to choose a group of able-bodied men and lead them in a counter-attack. Joshua's action was launched early next morning, and the ding dong battle continued throughout the day. Moses, accompanied by Aaron and Hur, climbed to the top of a hill which overlooked the battle-ground and gave directions by movements of "the rod of God in my hand". The Bible puts it: "Whenever Moses held up his hand, Israel prevailed; and whenever he lowered his hand, Amalek prevailed". Since his hands grew weary, Aaron and Hur supported his arms, and by sundown the Amalekites were routed.

The record of this engagement (in Exodus 17:8–14, with a valuable clue to Amalekite tactics in Deuteronomy 25:18) contains the first mention of Joshua. He had no doubt caught the eye of Moses on the latter's inspection visits, as Joshua was probably one

Now the house of Israel called its name manna   *(Exodus 16:31)*

This plant, common in Sinai, exudes a resin-like substance which, some botanists suggest, fits the biblical description of manna.

they could not drink the water of Marah because it was bitter; therefore it was named Marah (Exodus 15:23)

There were times, as at Marah, when the thirsty Israelites
came upon water and suffered bitter disappointment when they
found it to be brackish. Bedouin in Sinai today use
such water (on evaporation) as a source of salt.

of the clan or tribal marshals charged with getting the families ready for departure and shepherding them on the march. Moses must have marked him down as a bright and resolute young man, and sent for him in this moment of crisis. After his successful showing on the battlefield, he became Moses' personal aide and confidant — and ultimately his successor.

ADMINISTRATIVE REFORM

From Rephidim the Israelites pressed onwards into the peninsula and encamped near Mount Horeb, the place where, while tending Jethro's flocks, Moses had heard the voice from the burning bush. Learning that he was there, his father-in-law now paid him a visit, and it was during this visit that Moses decided to introduce a major reform in the basic system of public administration. The Bible ascribes the prompting of this move to the sage advice he received from Jethro; but it is also most likely that the Amalekite attack made Moses realise that the system of authority up to then had proved too weak, slow and cumbersome when challenged by a critical situation de-

manding quick decision and fast action. Under the patriarchal pattern prevailing before Moses appeared on the scene, authority had been wielded by the tribal and clan leaders, rather like Bedouin sheikhs in our own day, and their authority was considerable. With the arrival of Moses, supreme power passed to him, and he was able to exercise it because of his moral stature as the emissary of the Lord, his personal charisma and his undoubted talents of leadership. But he had to operate through the tribal and clan leaders, and these still commanded a good deal of independence. Since their offices were hereditary, they were not necessarily the ablest men in their groups; and since they enjoyed a measure of autonomy, and their interests were not always identical, cooperation was rarely automatic. This form of administration could no longer serve an embryo nation on its way through a treacherous desert and threatened now, as the Amalekite attack had shown, by surprise marauding raids. Later, no doubt, there would be more serious threats from full-fledged enemy armies. The patriarchal system had clearly to be replaced by something akin

108

to a military organisation, with the establishment of units which would correspond to today's section, platoon, company, battalion, brigade and division, and with a prescribed chain of command. This would also relieve the commander-in-chief, Moses, of many petty problems, which could well be delegated to junior officers.

The biblical account of the formation of this key administrative framework for the nation is told as part of the charming and apparently simple story of Jethro's visit to his son-in-law. The two men greeted each other warmly and spent the night reminiscing, with Moses telling about all the wondrous things that had happened since they had last met, and also, without doubt, something of the headaches and heartaches of leadership. In the morning, the sagacious old desert chief sat, watched and listened while Moses gave judgement in the disputes and claims brought before him. He saw the people milling around from morn to evening, awaiting their turn, and he heard how trivial were some of the complaints they brought. When Moses had done, Jethro said to him: "What you are

doing is not good. You and the people with you will wear yourselves out, for the thing is too heavy for you; you are not able to perform it alone. Listen now to my voice; I will give you counsel", and he urged Moses to delegate authority. He should "choose able men from all the people, such as fear God, men who are trustworthy and who hate a bribe; and place such men over the people as rulers of thousands, of hundreds, of fifties, of tens. And let them judge the people at all times; every great matter they shall bring to you, but any small matter they shall decide themselves; so it will be easier for you, and they will bear the burden with you." (Ex. 18:17–22.) Moses followed this advice, and took steps to select his senior and junior officers, from "rulers of thousands" down to commanders "of tens", who would exercise administrative authority under him. (It has been suggested by some scholars that this system made its appearance only centuries later, during the period of the Israelite monarchy; but many scholars hold that there is no reason to question its attribution to Moses.)

The introduction of this new administrative

The rising sun, taken from the summit of Mount Sinai. The Israelites were about to receive the Ten Commandments.

system would free Moses from routine duties, so that he could apply himself, under divine guidance, to moulding Hebrew society, framing their religious system and devising a code of ethics to guide their behaviour.

The climactic stage of the freedom trek through the wilderness was about to be reached — the handing down of the Law on the summit of Mount Sinai. This unique event was to shape the spiritual and physical lives of the Jewish people, stamp them with, and preserve, their special identity, and sustain them throughout all their vicissitudes in the millennia that followed. It was also to have a towering impact on a goodly portion of the human race as the key foundation of western civilisation.

110

The decorative doors of the Ark of
the Torah scrolls in the 19th century
synagogue of Mantua, Italy,
which were recently brought to the
Italian Synagogue in Jerusalem.
The tablet-shaped panels bear the
opening words, in Hebrew, of each of the
Ten Commandments.

3. THE LAW-GIVER

While the Israelites were encamped near the foot of Mount Sinai, Moses was called up to the mountain by the Lord, and the first phase of the covenant procedure was initiated. Moses was commanded: "Thus you shall say to the house of Jacob, and tell the people of Israel . . . if you will obey my voice and keep my covenant . . . you shall be to me a kingdom of priests and a holy nation". (Ex. 19:3–6.) Moses came down and relayed God's words, "And all the people answered together and said, 'All that the Lord has spoken we will do'." (Ex. 19:8.) When Moses returned to report the people's acceptance of the covenant, the Lord ordered that the Israelites should spend the next two days purifying themselves and on the third day he would come "in a thick cloud" to the mountain top and pronounce to Moses the text of the covenant so "that the people may hear when I speak with you, and may also believe you for ever". (Ex. 19:9.)

Dawn broke on the third day to "thunders and lightnings" and "Mount Sinai was wrap-ped in smoke . . . and the whole mountain quaked greatly".

DECALOGUE ON THE MOUNT

Amidst this awesome sound and sight, "God spoke all these words" — the Ten Commandments — "saying,

'I am the Lord your God, who brought you out of the land of Egypt, out of the house of bondage.

'You shall have no other gods before me.

'You shall not make for yourself a graven image . . .

'You shall not take the name of the Lord your God in vain . . .

'Remember the sabbath day, to keep it holy . . .

'Honour your father and your mother . . .

'You shall not kill.

'You shall not commit adultery.

'You shall not steal.

'You shall not bear false witness against your neighbour.

'You shall not covet your neighbour's

112

And he gave to Moses... upon Mount Sinai, the two tables of the testimony, tables of stone, written with the finger of God (Exodus 31:18)

A primitive 13th century painting from the Regensburg Pentateuch depicting successive sequences of Moses with the Tablets of the Law.

house ... or anything that is your neighbour's'." (Ex. 20:1–17.)

If, in the civilised world of today, it is taken for granted that killing is abominable, theft and adultery reprehensible, the worship of idols an abhorrence, the observance of the sabbath a vital safeguard of the health of the working population, it is due entirely to these landmark guidelines for human behaviour formulated three thousand three hundred years ago in the wilderness of Sinai. At the time they were startling and revolutionary, some of them marking an historic break from the customs and practices of the peoples of the ancient Near East among whom the Israelites dwelt. They represented a giant leap forward in the conception of man's relationship to man and to God, and so mighty an advance in the standards of human conduct that more than three millennia later they still command universal acceptance as the touchstone of civilised life.

But in the 13th century BC, it was something of a turning point, for example, to forbid sacred prostitution and ritualistic fertility orgies. The prohibition of man-made images for worship, when this was the common feature of all the faiths around them, showed the extraordinary courage of the extraordinary conviction of Moses and the Israelites that God was invisible, a spirit, an ineffable power. With polytheism rife, Israel was monotheistic. Where some contemporary religions approached monotheism by having a supreme god who was above all other gods, he nevertheless possessed a consort, a son, a daughter. The Israelite God stood alone. Where pagan gods were associated with a particular place, a mountain, a river, or with one of the elements, the Israelite God was everywhere, restricted to no special abode. And where the gods of some religions were identified with the sun or the moon, the God of Israel was the controlling power behind all the cosmic forces. All this, at that time, represented a new dimension in thought.

So staggering, indeed, is the idea of the sudden moral and religious enlightenment of Moses that the dramatic biblical account of the ceremony on Mount Sinai has been the subject of lively scholarly criticism. At the

114

Moses receiving the Tablets of the Law
on Mount Sinai. From the 13th century
illuminated Armenian Bible of Erzincan,
in the Library of St. Thoros, Jerusalem.

core of the criticism is not so much the
"thunders and lightnings" and the mountain
"wrapped in smoke" and quaking "greatly" —
though it is argued that Sinai knew no earth-
quake and its mountains were not volcanic —
as the fact that the supreme religious code
should have been sprung upon the Israelites
in the course of one stormy morning. The
most noted biblical critic of the 19th century,
the German scholar Julius Wellhausen (who
died in 1918 but who published his major
work before the turn of the century), concluded that it was "for the sake of producing
a solemn and vivid impression" that the
handing down of the Law on Sinai was
represented "as having taken place in a single
thrilling moment" when it really "occurred
slowly and almost unobserved". In the immediate decades that followed savants sought
to ascribe a later date to the origins of
Israel's faith.

Since then, however, the discovery of
further extra-biblical documents of the ancient
Middle East, more intensive research, and the
results of archaeological excavations have
convinced the leading modern biblical scholars
that the Decalogue and the covenant form of
the Sinai ceremony fit well with 13th century
BC convention, with the Mosaic tradition, and
with the social and political conditions of the
Israelite tribes. As biblical scholar John Bright
points out: "There is no reason whatever to
assume that Israel's faith fundamentally
changed with the settlement [in Canaan], or
gained its essential character after that event.
On the contrary, the evidence obliges us to
trace it in all its major lines back to the desert
and to Moses — who stands as the Bible
depicts him, as the great founder of Israel."

COVENANT TREATIES

The event on Mount Sinai is presented in the
Bible as a covenant or treaty-making ceremony
between God and the Israelites. We now
know, from recent studies of early Near
Eastern texts (notably the Hittite treaties of
the 14th–13th centuries BC), that in the time
of Moses, and earlier (as with the Patriarchs),
the covenant form was the established basis of
relationships between individuals, for example,
or between separate groups of people or
between an imperial overlord and a vassal

117

This church marks the site near Jebel Mussa where, according to an early Christian tradition, the Israelites fashioned the golden calf while Moses was away on the holy mountain.

state. In the case of the latter, it was usually stipulated that if the vassal respected his obligations, he would be protected; if he broke the covenant treaty, he would incur the overlord's wrath. There were also various types of covenant. The noted scholar George Mendenhall was the first to point out that the Sinai covenant followed the form of the suzerain-vassal type of treaty found in the Hittite texts. At that time, the Egyptians and the Hittites were the two great powers of the region, and the petty kingdoms were vassals of one or the other. These, by written treaty, were allowed to maintain their lands and kingdoms in exchange for the obligation to remain loyal to their masters. This was the very concept of the Israelite relationship to their suzerain. But there was this crucial difference: Israel's overlord was not a mortal king but God. Another noted scholar, the Hebrew University's Moshe Weinfeld, has shown that the idea of "the kingship of God" in the biblical covenants was unique in the 13th century BC Near East. And as against those scholars who had set this idea in a later century, Weinfeld makes clear "that God as king of Israel . . . is one of the most genuine and ancient doctrines in Israel" and that "Israel adopted the idea of the kingship of God a long time before establishing the human institution of kingship".

In the same way as the relationship between a regional power and a vassal kingdom would be formalised in a written treaty, so Israel's relationship with God had to be based on a written document. "No wonder", writes Weinfeld, "that the tables of the covenant played so important a role in the religion of Israel." In developing his theme, Weinfeld shows with illuminating insight that this was also why the Hebrew religion was the only one "that demanded exclusive loyalty" to God, "and precluded the possibility of dual or multiple loyalties, such as were permitted in other religions where the believer was bound in diverse relationships to many gods. So the stipulation in political treaties, demanding exclusive loyalty to one king, corresponds strikingly to the religious belief in one single, exclusive deity."

Thus, we see that at Sinai, though the content of the covenant was totally new, its form was in keeping with contemporary practice, and it was used precisely because it was familiar to the Israelites. We are told in the Bible that before the Commandments are given, Moses puts the Lord's proposal to the people. Do they accept a covenant? Yes, they answer. Then come its terms — the Decalogue. They hear and they accept. The covenant will then be put into writing. With that it becomes binding and a people with a specific identity is born.

George Mendenhall has observed that "the formation of a new legal community" — which was Moses' aim — "as well as the undertaking of new legal responsibilities, took place most naturally by covenant." And he adds: "The covenant at Sinai was the formal means by which the semi-nomadic clans, recently emerged from state-slavery in Egypt, were bound together in a religious and political community. The text of that covenant is the Decalogue." And these Commandments were "the source of community policy in law . . . the definition of right and wrong to which the community is bound."

Moshe Weinfeld, in a carefully reasoned

Fragments of a Torah scroll several hundred
years old in the possession of a Jewish
family in Peki'in, in Galilee, whose ancestors
escaped Roman attention in the 1st century AD
and remained in their village when most of
their compatriots were exiled. Peki'in has a
record of unbroken Jewish settlement
throughout the period of the exile.

study, writes that "The God, whose real name
Moses revealed to the children of Israel, was
not a new deity, but the God of their fathers,
who established a new relationship with them
by the act of redemption (Ex. 3:13 ff). The
purpose of the Sinai covenant was therefore not the acceptance of a new sovereign,
but the acknowledgement of a new system
of laws, which the liberation from slavery
and the achievement of political independence
made indispensable."

Albrecht Alt, in his important research on
Israelite law, has pointed out that the cate-
gorical imperatives and prohibitions in the
second person ("You shall not . . .") in the
Ten Commandments are very ancient in Israel
tradition and, with few exceptions, are unlike
the usual stipulations in other religions of the
ancient Middle East. Mendenhall has an
illuminating comment on the high number of
the Decalogue prohibitions — eight, as against
the two positive commands on the sabbath
and honouring parents. He sets them in the
context of the social and political make-up
of the Israelites. We have already seen that
the Israelite tribes and clans had been fairly

And he [Aaron] received the gold at their hand… and made a molten calf (Exodus 32:4)

The women brought their rings and bangles to Aaron, and he melted them down and shaped them with a graving tool into a golden calf (left). Desert women (right) to this day bedeck themselves with rings, bracelets and pendants.

Moses' anger burned hot, and he threw the tables out of his hands and broke them... (Exodus 32:19)

Rembrandt's Moses, depicted as he is about to break the Tablets of the Law, one of the most notable of the great biblical paintings by the 17th century Dutch master. The Hebrew writing on the foremost tablet is the text of Commandments 6 to 10.

autonomous, and the elders had enjoyed considerable independence before the arrival of Moses. To further his goal of liberation and building a free nation, he had to unite them, and this inevitably meant curtailing the authority of the tribal leaders. There had been opposition — the biblical record makes frequent mention of the "murmuring" of the people — and some of the elders must have resisted this crucial attempt to secure the general acceptance of a binding code. Such a code, however, was a prerequisite for unity. Thus, says Mendenhall, "For any set of stipulations to be acceptable" to men reluctant to see their autonomy infringed, "they would have to be of such sort that would correspond to the actual needs of a new community and guarantee them a maximum of self-determination . . . prohibitions only are universal, since they define only the areas which are not permitted, leaving all other realms of action free. A positive command, on the other hand, immediately excludes all other alternatives."

THE ORDINANCES

Exodus 19, which records the preamble and

preparations for the covenant, and Exodus 20, which presents the Ten Commandments (and which are repeated with certain textual differences in Deuteronomy 5:6–21), are followed in Exodus 21–23 by a series of ordinances, together with the penalties for infraction. These ordinances are varied and wide-ranging. A few deal with religious subjects, such as observance of the three main festivals, the tithing of the "first fruits", and the penalties for pagan worship and sorcery. Most, however, are secular, relating to crime, such as murder, theft, bribery, bestiality; to the treatment of slaves; to compensation for damage to life, limb and property; and to such moral guidelines, showing an extraordinary humaneness for those times, as "You shall not wrong a stranger or oppress him, for you were strangers in the land of Egypt"; "If you lend money to any of my people with you who is poor . . . you shall not exact interest from him"; and "If ever you take your neighbour's garment in pledge, you shall restore it to him before the sun goes down; for that is his only covering, it is his mantle for his body; in what else shall he sleep?"

124

This is the law which Moses set before the children of Israe

which Moses spoke to the children of Israel when they ca

ese are the testimonies, the statutes, and the ordinances,
it of Egypt... (Deuteronomy 4:44, 45)

One of the earliest Hebrew copies of the Ten Commandments discovered so far, written not later than the 1st century AD and possibly earlier. It is part of the biblical text on one of the Dead Sea Scrolls found in Qumran (Cave IV).

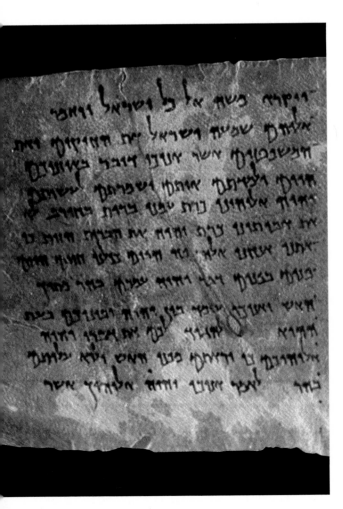

These three Exodus chapters are variously known as the Covenant Code or the Covenant Books. While all scholars agree that most of the ordinances in this code cover situations which well accord with the federal society of clans in the wilderness, some, it is argued, like damage by grazing beasts or by fire to cultivated "field or vineyard... or the standing grain", relate to conditions which were possible only after the settlement of the Promised Land. Some scholars reply that these ordinances were also projected into the future, and anyway such conditions could also have been possible during the long sojourn at Kadesh Barnea before the conquest of Canaan. However, particularly since the discovery of such codes of the ancient world as the 18th century BC Babylonian Code of Hammurabi and the 14th century BC Hittite Code, even those scholars who favour a later date for the Covenant Code agree that its origins reach back to more ancient traditions.

The purpose of Moses, guided by the Lord, in devising the Covenant Code was to put teeth into the Ten Commandments and add flesh to their bare bones. The Code is far

127

When Moses came down from Mount Sinai... the skin of his face shone because he had been talking with God

(Exodus 34:29)

The Moses of Michelangelo, a work of genius by the 16th century master, installed in the Church of S. Pietro in Vincoli, in Rome. Moses is represented with horns in his head because of a mistranslation. The Hebrew word for "horn" is similar to, and was mistaken for, the Hebrew word for "shone", which the Bible uses to describe Moses' glowing countenance as he descended from Mount Sinai.

more detailed, dealing with a host of situations likely to arise in human society. Moreover, the Commandments were straightforward stipulations representing "community policy" which bound the community but which contained no provision for their enforcement. This was done by the Code, and those parts of it which list the prohibitions carry the punishment for each. As Mendenhall has put it, if the Decalogue was "policy", the Code provided "those techniques of community action whereby these policies [were] served and protected".

Having mentioned these ancient codes of other nations, one must add that there have been a number of scholarly works which show, by a comparison with these early texts, how unique was. the Mosaic law We have space only for a few of the insights which emerge from Prof. Moshe Greenberg's study on biblical criminal law. He points out that whereas with the other codes the actual authorship is claimed by the mortal king — Hammurabi calls himself "the king of justice" and tells the people to "give heed to *my* precious words" — under the Mosaic code,

and indeed throughout the Bible, the idea of the transcendence of the law is given "thoroughgoing expression. Here God is not merely the custodian of justice or the dispenser of 'truth' to man, he is the fountainhead of the law, the law is a statement of his will." And "in the sphere of the criminal law, the effect of this divine authorship of all law is to make crimes sins, a violation of the will of God." What follows from this is a deep divergence between Israelite and Near Eastern law which "reflects a basic difference in judgments of value". In biblical law, as Greenberg points out, crime is an "absolute wrong", and the punishment must be appropriate to this principle alone. In the other codes, the penalties for crimes were determined by the political and economic exigencies of the community. Thus, certain types of theft carried the death penalty, whereas murder could be punished by placing an economic valuation on the loss of life. Under Assyrian law (14th–11th centuries), for example, the punishment of a murderer could take "the form of the surrender of other persons — a slave, a son, a wife, a brother — ... 'to wash

A grouping of idols from early historical periods on display in the Rockefeller Museum in Jerusalem. The concept of monotheism in Commandment One and the prohibition of worship of man-made images in Commandment Two were revolutionary and courageous in the idolatrous world of ancient times.

out the blood', or to 'make good' the dead person, as the Assyrian phrases put it. Equally expressive are the Hittite laws which prescribe that the killer has to 'make amends' for the dead persons by 'giving' persons in accord with the status of the slain and the degree of the homicide. The underlying motive in such forms of composition is the desire to make good the deficiency in the fighting and working strength of the community which has lost one of its members." This "view of life as a replaceable economic value" and where the "moral guilt of the homicide" is subordinated to the economic needs of the community "is the polar opposite of the biblical law", which holds that human life is unique and supreme. This "places life beyond the reach of other values. The idea that life may be measured in terms of money or other property... is excluded. Compensation of any kind is ruled out. The guilt of the murderer is infinite because the murdered life is invaluable ... The effect of this view is, to be sure, paradoxical: because human life is invaluable, to take it entails the death penalty. Yet the paradox must not blind us to the judgement

130

The 18th century BC stele
an 8-foot high stone mon
the great Babylonian kin
deity Marduk, and belo
in the Code of Hammurab
in Babylon and later r
(in Persia) where it was disc
It is now

of value that the law sought to embody." (Actually, post-biblical Jewish law was much troubled by this dilemma. However, it solved it in large measure not by following the other systems and substituting a financial punishment for the death penalty, but by setting such stiff, complicated and numerous conditions before a court could pass the death sentence, by showing, as Greenberg points out, such an exaggerated concern for "the life of the accused . . . that in effect it was impossible to inflict capital punishment".)

On the other hand, as Greenberg shows, both Assyrian law and the Hammurabi Code "know of offences against property that entail the death penalty. In Babylonia, breaking and entering . . . and theft from another's possession are punished by death; Assyrian law punishes theft committed by a wife against her husband with death. In view of this, the leniency of biblical law in dealing with all types of property offences is astonishing. No property offence is punishable with death".

Considering the unparalleled biblical leniency over property offences with its severity over murder, and the reverse attitude in the other Near Eastern systems, Greenberg writes that the "significance of the laws then emerges with full clarity: in biblical law life and property are incommensurable; taking a life cannot be made up for by any amount of property, nor can any property offence be considered as amounting to the value of a life." In the other codes, "the two are commensurable: a given amount of property can make up for a life, and a grave enough offence against property can necessitate forfeiting life." Thus, "a basic difference in the evaluation of life and property separates the one from the others. In the biblical law a religious evaluation, in non-biblical, an economic and political evaluation, predominates."

This is but an example of the profound values which lay behind the Sinai Commandments and the Covenant Code and their novelty at the period. They have become much clearer to us today as a result of modern discovery and research.

REBELLION

Following the initial Sinai ceremonies, Moses left Aaron and Hur in charge of the encampment and went up the mountain "with his servant Joshua". Called by God to receive "the tables of stone, with the law and the commandment, which I have written for their instruction" (Ex. 24:12), Moses left Joshua behind and disappeared into the cloud which covered the summit of Sinai. There he stayed forty days and forty nights communing with the Lord. While he was away, the people below urged Aaron to "make us gods", and Aaron fashioned a "molten calf" (Ex. 32:4) which they worshipped with sacrifices, feasting and pagan dancing.

What could have motivated this extraordinary action — and so soon after the covenant ceremony? The Bible says that the people approached Aaron when they "saw that Moses delayed to come down from the mountain", and they said: "as for this Moses . . . we do not know what has become of him". (Ex. 32:1.) The contemptuous words "as for this Moses" provide the principal clue to their thinking. It seems evident that as week followed week and Moses failed to appear, they came to believe that he was dead. In that case, all his grandiose promises

were clearly worthless. He had exerted his charismatic authority, sustained them with brave words, spoken as the emissary of God. But if he was no longer alive, he was probably not what he had claimed to be; or if he were, he had obviously been abandoned by the Lord. The covenant was no longer binding — it had in any case, as far as they knew, not yet been put in writing — and the laws were not valid.

The clan leaders who had resisted the limitation of their authority had no doubt been active in inciting their people; and they could have pointed to the suffering in the desert as a counter to the argument that Moses had, after all, liberated them from slavery. It must be remembered, too, that only about one year had passed since they had left Egypt. They had not yet shaken off their slave mentality and were a long way from being a united tempered group, steeled by a strong collective will. They were still a loose collection of clans who had responded to the call of this strong personality, Moses. But now he had disappeared — and there had not been time for him to train a level of

its frames, and put in its poles, and raised up its pillars;

d commanded Moses (Exodus 40:18, 19)

The consecration of the Tabernacle by Aaron
the High Priest, a scene from the biblical
frescoes in the 3rd century synagogue
of Dura-Europos in ancient Babylon.

leadership who could have taken over, nor time enough to put into effect the administrative reforms suggested by Jethro. Without him, the people felt helpless, forsaken, far from the homes they had left and with no compass for the future. They therefore resorted to the devices they had witnessed in Egypt when their neighbours had sought help in moments of anguish. (Some scholars hold that the golden calf suggested an association with Apis, the sacred bull of Egypt. Others say that they were really worsipping God, as witness Aaron's proclamation that there "shall be a feast to the Lord" and that only the external trappings of worship were Egyptian. Still others suggest that the entire episode is a later interpolation, designed to show the sinfulness of the golden calf worship instituted by King Jeroboam of Israel at Bethel and Dan.)

The Bible says that God had told Moses what was happening below and had threatened to destroy the people, but Moses pleaded for them and God relented. However, when Moses eventually came down the mountain and saw for himself what was going on, he

took "the two tables of the testimony ... tables that were written on both sides" — the written form of the covenant — "and broke them at the foot of the mountain." As Moshe Weinfeld points out, this again followed the accepted covenant procedure. Since "the written document expresses the validity of the given relationship", once the covenant was no longer in force, "the document must be destroyed. Thus, the worship of the golden calf which signifies the break of the Covenant is followed by the breaking of the tablets by Moses, the mediator of the Covenant ... Following the judicial pattern, the renewal of the relationship must be effected on the same basis, i.e. by writing new tablets ..."

DRASTIC ACTION

Arriving at the encampment, Moses quickly resolved that the most drastic action was called for if he was to reassert his control and pull the people together. He promptly burnt the golden calf, had it ground into powder, mixed it with water and forced the people to swallow it. He then rallied his own tribe of Levites and ordered them to put to

136

death a great number of the pagan worshippers.

His action was salutary. The people were contrite. And his authority was now greater than ever. His very reappearance had heartened the faithful, cowed the sceptics who had thought him dead, and discomfited those — probably disgruntled clan leaders — who had scoffingly spoken of "this Moses". Furthermore, upon his return, he had displayed a new side to his character, one they had not seen before, nor suspected. He was no longer the pleading leader, relying on persuasive words alone to secure their assent. He now showed that when necessary he could be ruthless. The people would not soon forget his swift judgement and action.

If until now they had respected his forceful tone, they would now also fear his iron hand. Not all, though most of them. Some of the discontented would continue their opposition. It would be muted for the time being under the impact of the trauma; but it would become sharper as a reaction to the more muscular leadership, and would eventually erupt into open conflict. But for the moment the people were subdued. And Moses could again make the ascent to the sacred mountain and again stay there forty days and forty nights, confident that they would not repeat their iniquitous breach of moral discipline.

He went up carrying two stone tablets he had freshly hewed to replace the ones he had broken; and when he came down, with "the words of the covenant, the ten commandments" (Ex. 34:28) newly engraved on the stones, Aaron and the Israelites saw that "the skin of his face shone", radiating such light that "they were afraid to come near him". (Ex. 34:30.) But he called them to solemn assembly and read out what had been written in the covenant.

(Visitors to the Church of S. Pietro in Vincoli, in Rome, admiring the celebrated Michelangelo sculpture of Moses, have wondered why he is represented with horns in his head. The horns are there because of a mistranslation of the Hebrew verse in the Bible describing Moses' glowing countenance as he descended Mount Sinai. The Hebrew for "shone" is "karan", written, since Hebrew is without vowels, as three consonants,

a very loud trumpet [shofar] blast, so that all the people who were in the camp trembled (Exodus 19:16)

Simchat Torah, Hebrew for "Rejoicing of the Law", is the last day of the Pilgrim Festival of Succoth, when Jews in olden times went up to the Temple in Jerusalem to demonstrate their joy in the Torah. Since the re-unification of Jerusalem, the festival can again be celebrated close to the Temple site (left), at the Western Wall. The sound of the shofar (below), the traditional ram's horn used in Jewish ritual, is again heard here.

"k r n", which could also be rendered, though in this context inaccurately, as "keren". This word has two meanings: "ray" and "horn", and "horn" was the word given in the Latin translation available to Michelangelo. The strange feature of his masterpiece is thus the product of a double literary lapse — the wrong reading of the Hebrew word and even that wrongly translated.)

During his first stay on Sinai, Moses had received from the Lord detailed instructions for building an ark of acacia wood covered with gold which would house the tablets of the Law. Aaron and his sons were to be ordained as priests to tend it. Moses now set the craftsmen among the people to build this Ark of the Covenant or Ark of the Law which would accompany the children of Israel throughout their journeyings.

4. MOULDING A NATION

It was now thirteen months since the Israelites had left Egypt, and they were ready to move on from the area of Mount Sinai towards their promised goal. Before doing so, however, Moses, always the farsighted statesman but now also the tough administrator, took two essential steps to turn his people into a cohesive force, deepen their feeling of group identity, tighten group discipline, and gear them to meet military challenges which, he envisaged, would be far graver than any they had encountered so far. He ordered a military census; and he prescribed a rigid marching order.

The census covered all able-bodied men from the age of twenty and upwards and was carried out by Moses and Aaron, tribe by tribe. In each tribe, they were accompanied by the tribal leader. The tribe of Levi alone was exempt, for the Levites would have charge of the Ark and all its accoutrements at all times, in peace and war, dismantling it and carrying the components on the move, assembling it at halts. The Bible, recording the result of the census, gives the total number of men "able to go forth to war" (Num. 1:46) as 603,550.

The order of march gave each tribe its assigned position, and this was coupled with a prescribed formation pattern whenever they pitched camp. They were organised in four sub-groups, each of three tribes, and when resting they would be ranged round all four sides of a square, one sub-group with its distinctive standard along each side. Judah, behind its tribal standard, together with Issachar and Zebulun, would encamp on the east; Reuben with Simeon and Gad on the south; Ephraim, Manasseh and Benjamin on the west; and Dan, Asher and Naphtali on the north. Each would thus be facing the compound, in the centre of which would stand the Tabernacle, the tent-like structure housing the Ark of the Covenant and the sacred objects, surrounded by the tents of the Levites.

At the order to move, Judah's sub-group would lead off. It would be followed by

Levites with the Tabernacle. Then would come Reuben's contingent, followed by other Levites carrying the Ark and the rest of the holy articles. After them would come Ephraim's sub-group, and Dan's contingent would bring up the rear. Within each tribe the clans were also given fixed positions. The signal to move and to halt would be given by trumpet blasts. The trumpet would also be used to sound a general alarm.

THE LONG SOJOURN

Following this new, disciplined march pattern, the tribal formations set off northwards, and for the next few months trekked slowly through the desert. This part of the journey was uneventful. They encountered no hostile bands, or if they did there is no record thereof. It is likely that since they were now better organised to meet the kind of attack they had suffered earlier by the Amalekite raiders, any marauding nomads on the hunt for prey would have been deterred. However, this did not mean that Moses could now relax. True, his administrative burdens were lighter with the appointment, under his reform plan, of re-sponsible subordinates. But as the Israelites trudged on day by day across the endless wastes of sand, tempers frayed and morale dropped. They bickered and they "murmured", grumbling about the pace, the heat, the cold, sickness, hunger and thirst. And it was Moses himself who had to deal with this general discontent.

It must be remembered that they were not like Bedouin whose life and future were bound to the desert and who had therefore created and accustomed themselves to a special design for desert living. For the Israelites, the wilderness was simply a stretch of arid terrain to be traversed as quickly as possible in order to reach and settle down in their promised land. If, to the desert nomad, each day was a challenge, to the Israelite it was a tiresome hardship, and as days extended to weeks and weeks to months, their mood grew more and more gloomy. It was with a sense of supreme relief that, two years out of Egypt, they arrived at the rich fresh greenery of Kadesh Barnea and Moses said they could rest. They could not know that they would be resting there for the next thirty-eight years — and for most of

the name of that place was called Kibroth-hatta'avah,
because there they buried the people who had the craving

(Numbers 11:34)

Ancient tombs recently discovered in southern Sinai, associated locally with Kibroth Hatta'avah (graves of the craving) of Numbers 11:34 where many Israelites died after indulging to satiety their craving for meat.

the older generation, the rest would be eternal.

Kadesh Barnea is a large oasis near the north eastern edge of the Sinai peninsula, some 50 miles south of Beersheba, at the southern entrance to the land of Canaan. They were now at the threshold to the promised land, but they knew nothing about that land. They knew that, unlike Egypt, with its settled boundaries and strong central authority, Canaan was a piece of territory which lay between the two rival empires of the age, with no defined frontiers and with no single all-powerful ruler, sparsely populated, with some of its inhabitants already settled in cities and villages and governed by a local "king", and others continuing the nomadic life, moving with their flocks in search of pasture and dwelling in tents.

INTELLIGENCE MISSION

So much Moses and the Israelites knew. But they needed to know very much more before they could attempt to enter this country. They needed to know the size of its mixed population, where each group was located, whether they were hostile or friendly, tough or easy-going, what kind of weapons they possessed and whether their cities were fortified. They also required information on its topography, climate, sources of water, and fertility.

There was only one way to find out — send in an intelligence team to carry out an unobtrusive reconnaissance. Being a political leader, instead of picking a random group, Moses chose one man from each tribe; being also a military leader, he made sure that each was an outstanding officer and respected by his tribe. (Joshua, for example, was selected to represent the tribe of Ephraim.) He then gave them their briefing, telling them "to spy out the land of Canaan" and to "Go up into the Negeb yonder, and go up into the hill country, and see what the land is, and whether the people who dwell in it are strong or weak, whether they are few or many, and whether the land that they dwell in is good or bad, and whether the cities that they dwell in are camps or strongholds . . . and whether there is wood in it or not. Be of good courage, and bring some of the fruit of the land." (Num. 13:17–20.)

The twelve-member reconnaissance unit left Kadesh and spent forty days on their mission, gathering intelligence on the key areas in the country. One item of their report was visible as soon as they entered the encampment on their return. It was a vine branch with a single cluster of grapes, so large that it was carried on a pole between two men. (It had been picked near Hebron.) This, plus pomegranates and figs, served to illustrate their unanimous judgement that the land "flows with milk and honey". (Num. 13:27.) But, their report added, its people were "strong", some of them "descendants of Anak" — Anak is the Hebrew for "giant" — and their "cities are fortified and very large". They then went into detail, noting that the hill country was held by Hittites, Jebusites and Amorites, but that the Amalekites held the Negev and the Canaanites the coastal plain and the Jordan valley.

The report was presented to Moses and Aaron at a general assembly. So far, it had been factual — the straighforward presentation of intelligence information — and it reflected the unanimous view of all twelve members of the team. Now came the implications of this factual material, and two members alone, Caleb, of the tribe of Judah, with the tacit support of Joshua, urged that they move north without delay — they were not many miles from the southern rim of Canaan — "for we are well able to overcome" opposition. But their ten colleagues expressed the other extreme, asserting that there was little hope, for the people they would be up against "are stronger than we" (Num. 13:31), and some of them were of such "great stature" that compared to them "we seemed . . . like grasshoppers".

This "giant" versus "grasshopper" presentation was so vivid that all who heard it were seized with fear and panic. Within minutes, pandemonium broke out, the people rising in anger against Moses for having brought them to this fearsome pass. He had deluded them, stringing them along with rosy promises of freedom, and all he could offer them now was the point of the enemy's sword. Canaan might be a fine country, but they would all be killed trying to get in. They would have been far better off had they refused to listen to Moses and stayed in Egypt. Someone even shouted above the clamour that they should choose another leader to take them back there.

The assembly was charged with tension, the mood combustible, and this was just the kind of proposal to spark a mutiny. In this critical situation, up jumped Joshua and Caleb, and, without repeating Caleb's suggestion that they proceed forthwith into battle, they tried to reassure the people that with God on their side they would overcome their enemies. They were almost stoned for their effort.

The Bible does not record how the meeting ended. It is likely, however, that, since there was no burning urgency for an immediate decision, they eventually dispersed, angry and bitter, thinking that they would continue the discussion among themselves on the morrow. Moses and Aaron probably retired to consult with Joshua and Caleb in order to review the military prospects in greater detail.

It may be wondered why a skilful leader like Moses would not have received the report of the reconnaissance unit privately instead of first hearing it in public. But he knew what he was doing. The fact is that he had specially

There were times during their first two years in the wilderness when the Children of Israel, encountering broad stretches of bleakness like this, stumbled over the parched and cracked surface with despair in their hearts.

drawn members of the unit from all the tribes to preserve communal harmony. Now that they were back, he would gain nothing by a prior meeting in privacy. If the majority report were adverse — as it turned out to be — he could not suppress it. Each member would go back to his tribe, be asked by his fellow tribesmen what he had seen and would tell them. This would produce despair, and it would soon be compounded by anger at Moses for having kept the news from them. The result would be a dangerous, sub-surface seething which would spread and finally erupt into violent anarchy and chaos. By arranging for a public presentation, though Moses could not have expected so disastrous a result, he at least had displayed good faith. True, his leadership was tarnished. But some of the tension had been released. The people had vented their rage. They were still furious with him, but perhaps after a little time tempers would be calmed.

The Bible says that because of the popular outburst, reflecting a lack of faith in the divine promises, God decreed that they would continue to wander in the wilderness until all the adults had died out, except for Joshua and Caleb. Only those who were now infants would be privileged to enter the promised land.

AN ABORTIVE FORAY

Meanwhile, at his consultations with Joshua and Caleb following the rowdy meeting, Moses must have come to the conclusion that an immediate invasion of southern Canaan, as Caleb had suggested, was not feasible. It was the shortest and most direct route, but it would bring them into immediate conflict with the entrenched Amalekites and Canaanites, and the Israelites were clearly in no position as yet to meet so powerful an enemy. Moreover, as the meeting had shown, their morale was so low that even if they had strength of muscle, they lacked the strength of will to engage in major battle. Action would obviously have to be delayed — long enough to train a vigorous army, one drawn from the young generation. (Ibn Ezra suggested that the "generation of the wilderness" who had experienced and become used to slavery was psychologically unsuited for the task of conquest.)

And the people of Israel ...stayed in Kadesh

(Numbers 20:1)

It was with supreme relief that the Israelites reached the sweet waters and fresh greenery of this spring at Kadesh Barnea, near the southern extremity of the Promised Land, and hoped that their trek was almost over. But they were to remain here for the next 38 years, and for most of the adults who had set out on the Exodus this was indeed journey's end.

Moses no doubt called the tribal elders next day and told them there would be no immediate move. They would remain in Kadesh for the time being, close to water and grazing grounds. Thus, they need fear no imminent encounter with the "giants".

This must have appeased the majority of the people. But there was one group who decided — possibly out of contrition for their behaviour the previous night — that it was worth trying a quick northern thrust. Moses sought to dissuade them, telling them that their effort "will not succeed" for they were "transgressing the command of the Lord ... for the Lord is not among you" and the Ark of the Covenant would not be with them. But they went nevertheless and were roundly beaten. After this unofficial — and abortive — attempt to invade Canaan from the south, the Israelites settled down to a life of nomadic herdsmen in the wilderness of Zin — northeastern Sinai and the northwestern Negev — with their base at Kadesh Barnea.

The report from the twelve intelligence scouts, the undisciplined reaction by the people, and

"...the people journeyed to Hazeroth". (Num. 11:35.)
"Hazeroth" is Hebrew for "fences", and here is an
unusual site of a fenced plantation in southern Sinai.

the unsuccessful foray by the impetuous dissident group convinced Moses that his planned schedule could never be met. He needed much more time to achieve a state of readiness in the community. He had been trying in the previous two years to unify them, tighten group discipline, raise their sights, instil ideals into them, fashion a religious and ethical code which they would honour, introduce an efficient administrative organisation. These were impressive goals, but hardly capable of being reached in so short a time even by a more assiduous and sophisticated group. Writing a law was not enough. The public had to be educated to understand, accept and respect the law, and this could not be effected over-night. The same principle held for a new administrative system, new customs, a new outlook. It took time for the people to change familiar patterns and adapt themselves to the new. Moses realised this now. Like all great leaders — whose very greatness lies in their being way ahead of their public — he had been impatient, always trying to force the pace, fighting against time. Now, at Kadesh, and during the decades that they remained

there, he set about with painstaking care to build the tribal federation into a close-knit, hardy, dedicated community, conditioned to meet the challenges of the future.

THE NEW GENERATION

He spent time guiding and training his subordinates, delegating more and more administrative authority. He developed the religious code, extended the civil laws, prescribed the rituals of worship, and specified the duties of the tribe with the special status, the priestly Levites. Permissiveness was gradually replaced by discipline and, when the time was judged ripe, there was stern punishment for infraction of the Covenant Code. The biblical account of this sojourn at Kadesh contains the first record of a man sentenced to death by stoning for "gathering sticks on the sabbath day" (Num. 15:32), a breach of the Fourth Commandment.

Execution of this sentence must have come as a shock to the community, and may well have touched off the revolt which is reported in the biblical chapter which immediately follows. The rising, led by Korah, Dathan and

It was from Kadesh Barnea that Moses sent the twelve scouts into Canaan, and this illuminated manuscript, the work of a Jewish artist and scribe in Egypt early in the 12th century, is devoted exclusively to the biblical account of their 40-day reconnaissance mission and intelligence reports.

152

Abiram, was supported by two hundred and fifty respected elders, all "well-known men" (Num. 16:2), some of them probably clan leaders who had never reconciled themselves to the clipping of their authority. They now rose up and directly challenged the leadership of Moses and Aaron. But Moses was now strong enough to crush the insurrection. In a dramatic example to the community, the Lord caused the earth to open and swallow up the rebel leaders, while their supporters were consumed by fire.

The only other outstanding event at Kadesh occurred during a drought when the people gathered before Moses in fierce complaint over the lack of water for themselves and their animals. The episode is similar to the one at Rephidim, described in Exodus 17. But whereas Moses had then been told by the Lord to strike the rock, he was now ordered to "tell the rock . . . to yield its water". Moses, uncharacteristically, acted as though he doubted the potency of God to "bring forth water" merely through words. He did not speak to it, but he struck it twice, and out gushed water in abundance. Weakness of faith in divine power, particularly by the leader of the people, was a grave sin, and the punishment was harsh. "Because you did not believe in me" (Num. 20:12), the Lord told Moses and Aaron that they would not be privileged to enter the Promised Land. (Their sister Miriam had died earlier at Kadesh.)

As the years went by, the infants who had been born and brought up in the wilderness and had never experienced serfdom in Egypt grew to manhood. Though there is no specific mention of it in the Bible, it is most likely, from the subsequent record, that these young men were now put through courses of military training, probably under the direction of Joshua. This was the generation which would be bearing the brunt of the fighting when they eventually crossed into Canaan. Here at Kadesh they could learn the preliminary skills of warfare. They would test their prowess in the engagements en route, so that by the time they reached the Canaanite border, they would be battle-worthy.

THE LAST LAP

The moment had come to leave Kadesh and

All twelve scouts were agreed on the bounties of the Promised Land, and brought back specimens of the magnificent fruits that grew there (and grow in Israel today), among them the nutritious and honey-sweet fig.

resume the movement towards their goal. The young generation was ready, but as yet untried, and Moses therefore decided against an attempted penetration of Canaan from the south, not wishing to risk a critical reverse at so early a stage. He opted instead for a longer route, one which would bring them to Canaan from the east, across the river Jordan. To reach this region most easily meant crossing the northern Negev to a point south of the Dead Sea, then moving northwards in Transjordan along the King's Highway, which was the main caravan route from the south to Damascus and Mesopotamia in the north. But this route lay through the lands of Edom and Moab, and Moses was as yet unwilling to face a major clash. He therefore sent messengers to the king of Edom seeking permission to cross his territory, undertaking to stick to the "King's Highway" (Num. 20:17) and to take no water from any of his wells — or to pay compensation if they did. The request was refused, and Moses decided on an even more lengthy detour. He first turned south, proceeding to Etzion Geber at the head of the Gulf of Eilat, and then swung round in

the land… flows with milk and honey, and this is its fruit. *(Numbers 13:27)*

The desert-worn Israelites also gazed with
delight at the luscious grapes (left),
so large that a single cluster had to be
carried on a pole slung between two men,
and at the exotic pomegranates (below),
their rich ruby juice held within ripened
skins of crimson and gold.

a wide arc and came north again, but now passing to the east of Edom. Some scholars hold that he bypassed Edom from the west and went right through Moab. The majority, however, favour the longer, circuitous route, holding that the Israelites, after bypassing Edom from the east, continued northwards along the eastern highlands, skirting the eastern edge of Moab, until they reached the Arnon river.

The territory to the north of this river was now being ruled by Sihon king of the Amorites, who had conquered it shortly before from Moab. Sihon's capital was Heshbon, roughly on the same latitude as Jericho but east of the river Jordan, so that access to the Jordan and to eastern Canaan lay through his territory. Moses accordingly sent the usual message to him requesting permission to pass through his lands. Sihon's response was a refusal, backed by an army which came out in full array to drive off the Israelites. But unlike their reaction earlier, when they had been refused by Edom and had simply turned and taken another route, the Israelites this time stood their ground, and in the actions

The wilderness of Zin, backdrop to Kadesh Barnea. When the time came to leave, Moses, unwilling to risk an immediate major clash by taking the direct route into Canaan, led his people on a lengthy detour, turning first south to the Gulf of Eilat and then swinging northeast into Transjordan.

158

the people of Israel... came into the wilderness of Zin
(Numbers 20:1)

which ensued, they defeated the Amorites. Though there had been some skirmishing en route, this was their first decisive battle, and in this inaugural military test, the new generation of Hebrews, better organised and better trained than their parents had been, proved their mettle. They routed Sihon's forces, shattered his regime, captured Heshbon and soon occupied his entire region, from the Arnon to the river Jabbok.

They then pressed on northwards into Gilead up to the river Yarmuk, and there they encountered and defeated Og, the king of Bashan. (Bashan is the territory north of the Yarmuk which is known today as the Golan Heights.) They now occupied the entire broad belt along the eastern bank of the river Jordan, and were bounded by Moab in the south and Ammon in the east. Here they remained for a while, consolidating their strength, improving their military organisation, occasionally dealing with incursions, like those of the Midianites. During this period, too, there occurred the episode of Balaam and his ass, when Balak, the king of Moab, deeply anxious about the strength displayed by the Hebrews in their routing of Sihon and Og, called upon Balaam the soothsayer to curse Israel and, instead, a blessing slipped out of his mouth: "How fair are your tents, O Jacob, your encampments, O Israel!" (Num. 24:5.)

Another census taken at this time showed that of all the men who had been in Egypt and had experienced the Exodus, only three were left alive — Joshua, Caleb and Moses himself. Aaron had died soon after leaving Kadesh on the summit of Mount Hor. Its location is not known.

MOSES' FAREWELL

The Hebrews would soon be taking the giant step for which the Exodus, the journey and the long sojourn in the wilderness had been but a preparation — entering the Promised Land. It would be fraught with danger, for although much of the land was empty, they could expect fierce opposition from nomadic groups who had preceded them and who were now entrenched in key localities. Thanks to Moses, they were ready to meet this challenge — and their destiny. It was he, under divine guidance, who had rallied their parents to resistance, broken their fetters, and led them safely through the desert, applying the skills he had acquired at Pharaoh's court and Jethro's encampment. He had been the mediator in the forging of God's Covenant with the people, framing a unique code of religious and ethical principles which gave them (and would preserve for all time) a specific identity. It was he who had moulded the varied groups of clans into an embryo nation, and laid the basis of a national discipline through the provision of a central legal structure and a central form of worship. And it was he who had kept alive the spirit of freedom, his eye fixed constantly on the goal of liberation, urging his people forward, at times gentle, at times ruthless, tending to their physical wants and stiffening their morale in moments of despair, seeking at all times to fill their hearts with his own sense of purpose.

His task was now done. He had lived long. He could look back on his years and discern the peaks of lofty achievement; but their slopes held shadows of sharp disappointment.

The gravest had stemmed from the illusion that promise and fulfilment could be spanned by the same generation, the generation of serfs. He had believed that they could march to his pace, be seized by his own visionary ideals and the burning urgency of his drive. Only at Kadesh had he come to understand that the formidable task of conquest and settlement was beyond the capacities of men and women whose will had been crushed by slavery. This was a task for the new generation, born free, hardened in youth by the toughness of desert life, who would battle an enemy with boldness and skill. He was wise enough to recognise that what he and the generation of bondsmen had done had been essential, and that, with all their shortcomings, it had been their extraordinary strivings and cruel sufferings which had brought their children within reach of the fruits. He and they together had laid the foundations of their freedom, their unique religion and their nationhood. It was now up to the young to meet the next crucial phase in the struggle for independence in their own land. He trusted them, was heartened by their strength of will and their readiness for

An inlet near Eilat which
the Israelites passed on
their journeyings, and
today a favourite picnic
and bathing site for
their descendants.

162

The Isle of Jezirat Fara'oun ("the Isle of Pharaoh") in the Gulf of Eilat, considered by a few scholars (though disputed by most) to be the original site of Etzion Geber which the Israelites reached after leaving Kadesh Barnea and from there turned and went north again.

self-sacrifice, and he had confidence in the man who would lead them — his successor would be Joshua. He had no doubt that, if they remained faithful to the Lord's covenant, they would prove equal to their task.

It was with these thoughts in mind that Moses gave his farewell addresses to the congregation of Israel. (They are recorded in the first person in the chapters of Deuteronomy.) To the children and grandchildren of those who had started the freedom march, Moses the educator recounted the drama of the Exodus and the journey through the wilderness, and exhorted them never to forget it. Moses the Prophet and Law-Giver recalled the Commandments and the Covenant Code and expanded the religious and legal statutes and ordinances. Finally, Moses the wise and experienced leader gave them guidance on their future behaviour when they came to settle in Canaan. He concluded his religious instruction with what have become the most noted words in the Hebrew Prayer Book, uttered to this day, after three thousand three hundred years, by Jews throughout the world: "Hear, O Israel: The Lord our God is one Lord; and you shall love the Lord your God with all your heart, and with all your soul, and with all your might. And these words which I command you this day shall be upon your heart; and you shall teach them diligently to your children . . ." (Deut. 6:4–7.) The injunction to teach "these words . . . to your children", faithfully followed through all the subsequent generations and centuries, is assuredly one of the reasons for Jewish survival — and for the regained State of Israel in our own day.

Moses then went up "unto the mountain of Nebo, to the top of Pisgah, which is opposite Jericho", and there he was given a view of the future Land of Israel. He looked out over the glorious panorama, below him the sparkling river Jordan flowing between rich green banks to the glittering Dead Sea, beyond it the plain of Jericho, and rising in the distance the plateau, the hills of Jerusalem and the central mountain range. He gazed in wonder at all that he saw, content that he had accomplished his part of the divine mission. He had brought his people this far, and he was hopeful for their future. But as he turned

they…encamped on the other side of the Arnon, which is…
Sihon king of the Amorites… fought against Israel. An

The Mountains of Edom, which
the Israelites bypassed from the east
by a circuitous route after the
king of Edom had refused them
permission to cross his territory.

...he boundary of Moab, between Moab and the Amorites...
...srael slew him (*Numbers 21:11, 13, 21, 23, 24*)

The plains of Moab. The Israelites skirted
their eastern edge and journeyed northwards
until they reached the territory of the
Amorites, and met them in battle. It was
their first decisive engagement.

When the ass saw the angel of the Lord, she lay down under Balaam; and Balaam's anger was kindled, and he struck the ass with his staff (Numbers 22:27)

Rembrandt's painting of Balaam and his ass. The soothsayer, sent by a panic-stricken king of Moab to curse the Israelites, set out on his ass, but on the way the animal balked. Though beaten, it refused to go on, for an angel with drawn sword hovered over the path. Eventually, when Balaam sought to curse the Israelites, he could voice only blessings.

to descend from the summit, there was sadness in his heart that for him the trek had ended, and that it would not be given him to enter what his eyes had been allowed to glimpse — the Promised Land.

There, "in a valley in the land of Moab", Moses died, "but no man knows the place of his burial unto this day". (Deut. 34:6). It is still not known, though it must be in the vicinity of Mount Nebo, some 7 miles beyond the northeastern edge of the Dead Sea. There can be no doubt that the concealment of his sepulchre was deliberate, to avoid its becoming a cultic site, venerated as a sacred shrine, which might have led to the deification of this man of such prodigious stature: "And there has not arisen a prophet since in Israel like Moses, whom the Lord knew face to face." (Deut. 34:10).

He was mourned for thirty days, and then the children of Israel, under Joshua, girded themselves to cross the Jordan — and fight the first Jewish War of Independence.

5. THE PROMISED LAND

The process of conquest was long and tough. The strategy of penetrating Canaan from the east was sound, for this region was less thickly populated and less stiffly defended than the southern coastal plain. But it still offered formidable obstacles, notably walled cities, to the poorly armed Israelites who lacked the standard military resources of the period, such as battering rams, to overcome them. Nevertheless, the people enjoyed several advantages which were to prove decisive. They were led by Joshua, and Moses had chosen well when he had spotted this young man early on during the wilderness trek and picked him as his aide; for Joshua was to prove an ingenious military commander — a wise strategist, a resourceful tactician and a daring fighter — as well as a magnetic popular leader. Moreover, the forces he commanded were united as they had never been before. This was due partly to the efforts of Moses in the immediately preceding years. A more important reason was that the people were now at war, committed, as they knew, to

continuous battle for many years ahead, and a people is always more united in war than it is in peace. But perhaps the principal factor, which was to be even more crucial during the settlement period, is that all were bound by a covenant with God, by a distinctive faith, and this made the Israel experience so very different from that of other infiltrating nomadic tribes — and gave it a lasting impact. They were a more cohesive force than the enemies they faced and were moved by a higher sense of purpose, and they accordingly displayed a more tenacious fighting morale. It was their unique faith, as John Bright says, "which set Israel off from her environment and made her the distinctive and creative phenomenon that she was."

JOSHUA THE WARRIOR-LEADER

As a member of the 12-man reconnaissance team sent by Moses, Joshua knew something of the terrain he was about to encounter. But he now required up-to-date intelligence, and he needed information particularly on

Moses went up ... the Lord showed him all the land ... And ... said ... I will give it to your descendants (Deuteronomy 34:1–4)

It was across the easily passable fords of the narrow river Jordan (below) that the Israelites would enter Canaan. Looking westwards, Moses could see the mountains of Ephraim (right), the central range of the future Land of Israel which he was allowed to view but which he would not live to enter.

Remains of fortifications of various settlement periods discovered at archaeological excavations of the ancient site of Jericho, the first city in Canaan conquered by Joshua. The circular tower (centre) belongs to the Neolithic period.

the defences of Jericho — the first major obstacle astride his route of advance — and on its state of morale. He accordingly sent in a small unit — two men — to infiltrate the city and report back. They made their way across the narrow river at night, probably cut across westwards beyond Jericho, and entered the city in the morning by the west gate, giving the impression that they had come from the interior of the country. They wandered round the city — travellers were not uncommon — keeping their eyes and ears open, and arranged to lodge in the house of Rahab the harlot, conveniently "built into the city wall". (Josh. 2:15.) They were no doubt expert at gathering intelligence but not at doing so unobtrusively, and they excited the suspicion of the authorities, who came to Rahab's dwelling looking for them. However, the spies must have taken Rahab into their confidence and gained her trust, and, at her suggestion, had slept not in a room but on the roof, hidden among the stalks of flax. When the officials called, Rahab fobbed them off with the tale that the men had come and gone, she did not know where, but if they were

promptly pursued they would be overtaken. Later that night, she let them down by a cord over the outside wall, and they made for the mountains, hiding there for three days before returning to report their findings to Joshua.

Shortly afterwards, Joshua gave the order to move. The people crossed the Jordan at a small ford just north of the Dead Sea, in good order and without opposition, and proceeded to Gilgal, which lies between the river and Jericho. Here they set up their base and here, for the first time in Canaan, the Israelites celebrated the Passover Festival. Nothing could have better served to fortify their spirits than this ritual recollection of the Exodus and their divine liberation from bondage. So far, the Lord's promises had been fulfilled. They had entered the Promised Land. True, there was grim fighting ahead, but they could face it with the profound conviction that they would emerge the victors. It was a fit and courageous body of fighters, filled with religious zeal, who set out shortly afterwards for Jericho.

The collapse of Jericho's walls amidst the trumpeting and shouting on the seventh day

172

Panoramic view of the city and plain of Jericho, looking east. The long ridge in the upper part of the photograph is the ancient mound of Jericho.

(Josh. 6:20), after the Israelite forces had silently marched round the city on each of the previous six days, was probably less of a surprise to Joshua than it has been to some modern Bible critics. But, unlike these critics, Joshua was able to gauge — and had clearly devised his plan in the context of — the differing morale in the rival forces. The Bible does not record the words of the two intelligence officers who reported to him after their mission to Jericho; but it is reasonable to suppose in the light of the preceding and subsequent events that they had found the men of Jericho in a state of alarm. They would certainly have heard of the extraordinary Israelite victories over the Amorites and Bashanites across the river. They would then have witnessed the strange and frightening sight of the Israelites crossing the Jordan. (Even today, from the ramparts of ancient Jericho one has a clear view of the river across the low-lying plain.) They would have seen them moving forward to encamp at Gilgal, and begun to wonder whether they would bypass, or make straight for, Jericho. They would then have recalled that some weeks

Jar in the shape of the head of a Canaanite, belonging to the 16th century BC, discovered at archaeological excavations in Jericho.

earlier there had been two strangers inside their walls who had escaped and eluded the pursuit party. Just as it would have dawned on them that the two men must have been Hebrew spies, they would suddenly have spotted the Israelite force moving towards them. Knowing what had happened to the kings Sihon and Og, they must have been filled with despondency; but they had no doubt found reassurance in the strength of their walls.

STRATAGEM IN BATTLE

Since Joshua possessed none of the means to scale, tunnel under or breach their ramparts, he had to strike at their weakest point — their morale. This was the one factor in which his own force outmatched the men of Jericho, and he accordingly conceived an attack plan suited to the circumstances. Where today an enemy might be subjected to a preparatory "softening" by an artillery barrage, Joshua "softened" them by psychological warfare, using a stratagem to lull them into a false sense of security and then springing his surprise. (This theory is suggested by the archaeologist Yigael Yadin, and he writes that the psychological warfare stratagem reported in the Book of Joshua "is explicable in the light of a later one which is described in a Roman book of military ruses composed by Frontinus".) What Joshua had done was to parade his men silently round the walls on the first day, and this had made the Jericho defenders nervous and confused. Doing the same on the second day had still kept them guessing. By the end of the third day they had begun to relax their vigilance. By the fourth and fifth they may well have thought that the Israelites were indulging in a harmless drill. By the seventh, expecting the "drill" to end as before, the men of Jericho were startled by the shouting and trumpeting and panicked when the Israelites suddenly broke ranks and began rushing the walls. The defences collapsed. Ramparts often produce a passive mentality, and it had not occurred to the men of Jericho to defend their city by leaving it earlier and marching forth to try to prevent the Israelites from crossing the river Jordan.

The Jericho victory may have made Joshua

over-confident and his men less wary. Their next target which lay along their route to the central hills was the city of Ai, and a reconnaissance patrol reported that it was lightly held. This proved to be poor intelligence and when a small force was sent up the slopes to storm it in the conventional manner, it was repulsed. This sobering experience warned him and his men to be vigilant at all times in a situation of war, and reminded the commander that so long as he was without the means of penetrating fortified ramparts, he had still to resort to stratagems. He had also to concentrate a larger force.

Again, the plan he devised showed resourcefulness as well as the ability to predict the enemy's reactions to certain initial moves. If he could not batter the walls, he had to induce their defenders — unlike those at Jericho — to abandon them. He therefore sent a unit up the mountain under cover of night with orders to take up concealed positions behind the city — between Ai and Bethel. In the morning, Joshua with his main force appeared in front of the city, and, after the first engagement, they turned tail and

Remains of the ancient city of Ai, the second fortified city which Joshua took, after an initial reverse, by military stratagem.

So Joshua arose, and all the fighting men, to go up to Ai (Joshua 8:3)

The execution of the king of Ai (above); and Joshua's reception of the Gibeonite delegation who had come disguised as weary travellers from a distant land (below). From an illuminated manuscript in the Pierpont Morgan collection.

simulated flight. The people of Ai, contemptuous of the Israelites whom they had sent packing a few days earlier and who seemed now again to be on the run, promptly pursued them, as Joshua judged that they would. He and his men continued their flight, drawing the forces of Ai further away from their city. Suddenly Joshua flashed a signal — by waving his spear — to the unit lying in ambush, and they rushed into the now undefended Ai and set it alight. When the pursuers looked back and saw the smoke rising from their city, they were dumbfounded — and they were even more shocked when Joshua's forces, who had seemed to be in full flight, abruptly stopped, turned, and fell upon them. (This classic military ruse is recorded in Joshua 8.)

Not every engagement was based on military wile and not every battlefield was a fortified city. There was also a good deal of tough, conventional fighting in open terrain, and the Israelites became stronger, more confident, more skilful, more seasoned with each battle. Their military successes also served to weaken the morale of potential enemies, and not a few sought hasty pacts with Joshua to avert an armed clash. One of them was a federation of four cities, headed by Gibeon, who secured their alliance by trickery.

The Gibeonites inhabited the hill-country a few miles northwest of Jerusalem, and they dominated the route down into the lowlands through the valley of Aijalon. This was the obvious route of advance which Joshua would be taking to reach the coastal plain, and he would assuredly seek to protect his movement down the defile by first eliminating possible attack positions on the heights. Fearful of annihilation by the victor of Jericho and Ai, the Gibeonites resorted to a ruse. They sent a large delegation of elders and others, disguised as travellers who had been on a long journey, to Joshua's base at Gilgal. Their garments were old and threadbare, their sandals worn, their wine-skins patched, their bread dry and mouldy, their asses covered with old sacks. "We have come from a far country", they told Joshua, for they had heard of his military wonders under the guidance "of the Lord your God", and sought his friendship; "so now make a covenant with us." (Josh. 9:6.) Some of Joshua's aides

180

היה מלך גבעוניה כי כבלא אורבן עשה יהושע כי יעשון איען כי יעשון רא עירון ואר

habita audita restructione cinitatum hierico. 7 hai. tpls Gabaon priinus malicose cegirunt ne
ad Josue dissimulantes q esset illarum regionum incolla. et quasi uenient de longinquo in einus
sigurn acceperunt uestes antiquas. et fractos calceos. et panes puetustes. atqz in uenienes ad exeri
tum nostru. p huiusmodi cautelam fecerunt cum eo fedus ut securi essent. nec occiderentur ab eo

The central area, later settled by the tribe of Benjamin, between the hills of Judah and the mountains of Ephraim, which was the scene of Joshua's early battles.

were sceptical, and wondered whether they did not perhaps live in the vicinity; but the delegation pointed to their tattered clothing and dry victuals — which had been fresh when they had set out but had rotted during the lengthy travel from their distant land. They were very convincing and Joshua believed them, granting them a treaty of friendship with the specific stipulation to spare their lives. The covenant was sealed with solemn oaths.

Three days later the Israelites discovered that they had been tricked, and they promptly marched on Gibeon. The culprits were contrite, explaining to Joshua that they had been prompted by fear, and asking forgiveness. "We are your servants . . .", they told him, "and now, behold, we are in your hand: do as it seems good and right in your sight to do to us." (Josh. 9:8, 25.) His people were angry, but Joshua insisted that an oath was an oath, and the Gibeonites were not harmed. However, as a punishment for their guile, Joshua told them that henceforth they would be "hewers of wood and drawers of water for the congregation and for the altar of the Lord". (Josh. 9:27.)

In making a pact with Joshua, the Gibeonites had acted independently. They had thereby rejected the plea of the various Canaanite rulers to form a coalition and join in united battle against the Israelites. Their defection now left the cities in southern Canaan exposed, and the local kings were incensed with Gibeon — and alarmed by Joshua. The king of Jerusalem thereupon called upon the rulers of Hebron, Jarmuth, Lachish and Eglon, to ally themselves with him in a league of five cities and march on Gibeon, "for it has made peace with Joshua and with the people of Israel". (Josh. 10:4.) They agreed, and the five allied forces moved north through the hills and took up siege positions round Gibeon and its three other federated cities. The Gibeonites sent urgent appeals for help to Joshua, citing their treaty of mutual friendship. Joshua kept faith, seeing also opportunity in the challenge, and led his men on a night march from Gilgal. He took the attackers by surprise — he "came upon them suddenly" (Josh. 10:9) — and assaulted them simultaneously at different points. They were thrown into confusion, and rushed in head-

183

The dagger (centre), javelin-head (extreme left)
and spear-head (second from right), discovered
at archaeological excavations, were in use during
the period of Joshua's conquest. (The other two
weapons belong to the period of the Patriarchs.)

long retreat down the mountains through the
descent of Beth-Horon into the vale of Aijalon,
with the Israelites in hot pursuit. The five
kings and their fleeing soldiers were further
afflicted by the weather, running into a violent
hail-storm: "there were more who died
because of the hailstones than the men of
Israel killed with the sword". (Josh. 10:11.)
Darkness was now approaching, and Joshua
was afraid that they might either get away
or regroup under cover of night and stage a
counter-attack. He appealed to the Lord for
deliverance: "Sun, stand thou still at Gibeon,
and thou Moon in the valley of Aijalon".
(Josh. 10:12.) The five kings were killed, their
armies vanquished.

The way to the south was now open, though
Joshua prudently bypassed the strong fortresses of Gezer and Jerusalem (despite the
death of its king), and advanced into the
southern coastal plain. Following the astute
military strategy of first subduing the string
of fortresses which commanded the approaches
to the southern hill country, he conquered
Makkedah, Libnah, Lachish and Eglon in

rapid succession. This left him a clear route
through the passes and he now wheeled east
to assault and capture the important hill-city
of Hebron. He concluded this phase of his
southern fighting by turning back to the
southwest and taking Debir.

Only the north of the country remained to
be conquered and Joshua moved his army
towards Galilee. The most powerful ruler in
the region was the king of Hazor, and, at the
approach of the Israelites, he gathered together the neighbouring rulers and their
armies and all were resolved to face the
impending danger with joint action. Their
strategy was to go forth to meet and vanquish
Joshua in open battle before he had the chance
to come up to their cities and pick them off
one by one. The contending forces clashed in
ferocious combat "at the waters of Merom"
(Josh. 11:5), and Joshua's men, by now the
most battle-hardened veterans in the country,
routed the allied forces. Joshua then proceeded to Hazor itself, overlooking the Huleh
Valley and commanding an important stretch
of "the way of the sea", the main road from
Egypt to Damascus. Though heavily fortified,

it failed to resist the onslaught of the Israelites and was destroyed.

Joshua had fashioned a great army, and had led it through successful campaigns with consummate generalship. By the time he died, the Israelite tribes were firmly established in the land.

It is evident, however, both from certain passages in the Book of Joshua and from the whole of Judges, that the conquest was not completed in Joshua's time. The extreme north of Canaan — the territory now known as Syria and Lebanon — as well as the coastal plain remained unconquered. And several strongholds in the centre, like the cities of Jerusalem and Gezer, remained enemy enclaves within Israel. But as a result of Joshua's actions, the tribes would eventually gain mastery over the entire land and develop their distinctive national life.

THE ARCHAEOLOGICAL EVIDENCE

Attempts by biblical critics to downgrade Joshua's achievements — suggesting that the capture of certain cities ascribed to him was in fact effected only in the course of the following two centuries — have been definitely countered by recent archaeological discoveries. The most dramatic were the finds by Yigael Yadin at his excavations at Hazor from 1955 to 1959. "Joshua turned back at that time, and took Hazor, and smote its king with the sword; for Hazor formerly was the head of all those kingdoms . . . and he burned Hazor with fire." (Josh. 11:10, 11.) Yadin found that Hazor was indeed huge, by the scale of the times, and well meriting the title "head of all those kingdoms". But he also brought to light the remains of a well-built Canaanite city, with houses and a canalization system, whose floors were littered with the Mycenaean type of pottery definitely belonging to the 13th century BC. The thick layer of ashes showed that this (lower) city was destroyed by fire and never re-settled. This discovery not only supports the text of Joshua but also settles for all time the problem of dating the conquest. This had been the subject of much controversy, several scholars holding, on the basis of archaeological knowledge — as well as faulty interpretation — up to then, that Joshua's appearance in Canaan occurred in the 14th century BC. It is now clearly seen to have happened in the 13th century.

The archaeological evidence at Jericho seems indeterminate. Up to quite recently it was thought to be negative because the remains of the ancient wall closest to the period of Joshua were found to belong to an earlier age. But part of this wall may have been standing in Joshua's time, and there are pottery discoveries which are not inconsistent with a 13th century destruction.

Lachish (Josh. 10:32) — as we know from the inscription on a bowl found among the archaeological remains of the last Canaanite city on this site — fell on or about the year 1220 BC — consonant with the dates of Joshua. Debir (Josh. 10:38), also called Kiriath-Sepher (Josh. 15:15), was found through archaeological excavations to have been destroyed at the same time.

Throughout his campaigns, Joshua the military commander never forgot that he was also successor to Moses, and he showed an equal concern with the religious and ethical development of the people. Shortly after the battle for Ai, he assembled them on the slopes of Mounts Ebal and Gerizim, above Shechem, and "he wrote upon the stones a copy of the law of Moses . . . And afterward he read all the words of the law, the blessing and the curse, according to all that is written in the book of the law. There was not a word of all that Moses commanded which Joshua did not read before all the assembly of Israel . . ." (Josh. 8:32–35.) Joshua held repeated gatherings of this kind, urging the people to "take good care to observe the commandment and the law . . . to love the Lord your God, and to walk in all his ways . . . and to serve him with all your heart and with all your soul". (Josh. 22:4.) Concerned lest they adopt the customs and faith of their neighbours, he exhorted them not to "be mixed with these nations . . . or make mention of the names of their gods, or swear by them, or serve them, or bow down yourselves to them, but cleave to the Lord your God . . ." (Josh. 23:7, 8.)

TRIBAL SETTLEMENT

With the campaigns over, the time had come for the tribes to start settlement of their

Sun, stand thou still at Gibeon, and thou Moon in the valley of Aijalon
(Joshua 10:12)

The Valley of Aijalon, roughly midway between Jerusalem and Jaffa, where Joshua bade the moon stand still so that the retreating armies of the five kings who had attacked Gibeon should not escape under cover of the approaching darkness.

designated areas. Reuben, Gad and part of the tribe of Manasseh had been allowed by Moses to take title to the lands in Transjordan which had been conquered before the crossing of the Jordan. He had stipulated, however, that their able-bodied men join the other tribes in the coming battles for Canaan, and only at the end of the war would they return to their families. They could now do so. Judah was allotted the land south of Jerusalem. Ephraim and the other part of Manasseh, the tribes of the sons of Joseph, were given the areas south and north of Shechem in the centre of the country. The rest of the land was divided by lot among the remaining seven tribes. Included in the distribution, for future settlement, were areas not yet subdued. The lots were drawn at a special assembly at Shiloh.

It was at Shiloh, located some twenty miles north of Jerusalem, that Joshua had "set up the tent of meeting" (Josh. 18:1), and this was to remain the centre of worship for almost the next two centuries. Shiloh was thus the first site of Jewish pilgrimage (to be superseded by Jerusalem when David brought the Ark

of the Law there at the beginning of the 10th century BC), and at first, tribal representatives would assemble there. Later, "the whole congregation of the children of Israel" would gather there in fulfilment of the original injunction in Exodus (23:17 and 34:23) and in Deuteronomy 16:16: "Three times a year all your males shall appear before the Lord your God at the place which he will choose: at the feast of unleavened bread [Pesah], at the feast of weeks [Shavuot], and at the feast of booths [Succoth]."

It was at Shechem, however, that Joshua held a solemn assembly and within the sanctuary of the city "made a covenant with the people that day, and made statutes and ordinances for them ... And Joshua wrote these words in the book of the law of God". (Josh. 24:25, 26.) (Chapter 24 in the Book of Joshua is regarded by scholars as perhaps the most authoritative passage on Israel's covenant tradition which continued from the period of the Patriarchs up to the second Commonwealth.) This ceremony at Shechem was a renewal of the Sinai covenant, and Moshe Weinfeld suggests that one of its

principal aims was to check the danger of paganism. This threatened to spread with the development of friendly relations between the Israelites and the local Shechemites, who, for their own security, wished to live in peace with Israel. Many, indeed, had adopted the Israelite religion, without, however, abandoning their pagan deities, and their rites could well have proved contagious. Joshua was determined to stamp them out.

The biblical record shows that the Israelites quickly began settling and developing the land with the same energy with which they had fought for it, and this is borne out by the archaeological evidence. As William Foxwell Albright writes: "Archaeological excavation and exploration are throwing increasing light on the character of the earliest Israelite occupation, about 1200 BC. First it is important to note that the new inhabitants settled in towns like Bethel and Tell Beit Mirsim (Kiriath-Sepher) only a short time after their destruction. The Israelites were thus far from being characteristic nomads or even seminomads, but had reached a stage where they were ready to settle down, tilling the soil and dwelling in stone houses. A second main point is that the new Israelite occupation was incomparably more intensive than was the preceding Canaanite one. All over the hill-country" — which was their main region of settlement in this early period — "we find remains of Iron Age (12th century) villages which had not been inhabited in the Late Bronze Age (15th–13th centuries) and many of which had never been occupied previously."

THE CONFEDERACY

With the death of Joshua, there passed from the Israel scene the figure of a central leader who could command supreme authority over all the tribes and hold undisputed office for a long period. This leaderless situation reflected a strange irony in this initial period of settlement: that after all their sufferings and achievements, the community had returned to the state of tribal autonomy they had lived under in Egypt and the early years in the wilderness. They subscribed to no ordered system of central administration, had no political capital, maintained no central military organisation. Each tribe, now settled in its own tribal area, was preoccupied with developing and adapting to the new pattern of life in its own region, with no urgent immediate concern for the welfare of the other tribes. Their own tribal society was once again largely patriarchal, with justice within the clan or tribe dispensed by the tribal elders in accordance with tribal tradition. Thus, while Moses had sought to unify them and Joshua had succeeded in doing so during the war years, it would seem that they had now disintegrated into their former twelve fragments, each a world unto itself.

But there was this crucial difference: because of the dramatic ceremony at Sinai, they were now a confederation of tribes bound together and united in their collective covenant with God. And added to their common faith was of course the common memory of the awesome wonders, divinely ordained, of their immediate past. Whatever the degree of civil autonomy enjoyed by each tribe, all looked up to the central shrine which housed the Ark of the Covenant, and Shiloh, for most of the post-Joshua and pre-monarchic period, was the focal point of the confederacy. Here the

And Joshua turned back...and took Hazor...for Hazor formerly was the head of all those kingdoms *(Joshua 11:10)*

A basalt orthostat (left) bearing a relief of a lion, and steles, stone monuments, discovered in the remains of a 14th–13th century BC Canaanite temple at Hazor. Remains of a public building (right) also discovered at Hazor. In the periods of settlement subsequent to Joshua's conquest, only the upper city of Hazor was rebuilt.

tribal elders would meet at festival times and use the occasion to exchange views on common problems, possibly clear up disputes and perhaps agree to a limited cooperation on matters of mutual interest.

In the early years, however, such exchanges were informal and rarely led to any common policy or action of major degree. For at that time, soon after the conquest, there was no serious military danger, and each tribe could cope on its own — through its own tribal militia, made up of warriors drawn, by a quota system, from each family and clan — with the occasional small-scale raids by marauding nomads. The tribal elders were pleased to regain the kind of authority such leaders had not enjoyed since the days before Moses, and each tribe ploughed its own furrow. Indeed, it was often so anxious to further its individual tribal interests that it occasionally found itself in conflict with the material interests of tribes with whom it shared common boundaries, and the Bible provides a record of several grim and quite bloody inter-tribal clashes.

Within a few years, however, the phenomenon of inter-tribal cooperation was to reappear, albeit sporadically, brought about by the incursions of new and vigorous enemies as well as by old enemies who had regained their strength. These threatened the very existence of all the tribes, and this menace fuelled the process, lengthy as it was, of hammering them into national unity. In the second half of the 12th century BC came the Philistines from the Aegean region, a hardy energetic people who settled in the coastal plain and sought, in time, to press inland. Then came the Midianites who, as Albright points out, "had learned how to use the recently domesticated camel with terrifying effectiveness in long-range raids". There was trouble from those Canaanite city-states which had not been subdued; from the Aramaeans who infiltrated from the Syrian desert; and from the kings of Moab and Ammon on the other side of the Jordan whose passive hostility in the time of Moses had become overt. Some of these peoples had begun to consider that they stood a good chance of overwhelming the Israelites by gobbling them up tribe by tribe.

Fortunately for the Israelites, they usually—though not always — managed to perceive the hazards in time, and in moments of acute crisis all, or several, of the tribes would sink their differences, merge their interests and do battle for the common cause, rallying behind an *ad hoc* leader. Such spontaneous leaders were known as Judges, and they would call upon the people to discharge their obligations under the covenant and rouse them to fight for the survival of the whole community and the preservation of their faith. These Judges enjoyed no formal or absolute authority. They could apply no sanctions — beyond a curse — if any tribe failed to respond (as some did). Nor was their authority permanent: it usually lasted only during the period of grave danger (though in some cases it was extended). In such periods, the confederacy of tribes took on the aspect almost of a united nation, and their proclaimed commander that of a national leader. As soon as they felt the danger had passed, the people reverted to the autonomous tribal pattern and the leader ceased to wield national authority. What usually followed was a period of religious laxness in which the temptations of the customs and worship of their pagan neighbours often proved stronger than the call of Shiloh. Thus, in times of quiescence, as the Bible laments, "there was no king in Israel; every man did what was right in his own eyes". This moral laxness was frequently accompanied by a dangerous relaxation of vigilance, which would be ended by a further critical threat of attack — and the spontaneous choice of another Judge.

The Judges were not drawn from any special tribe, nor from any particular social stratum. (Jephthah was "the son of a harlot". Jud. 11:1.) Some had not even been leaders of their own tribes. Not all were men — one of the most outstanding was Deborah. Some had become widely known for individual feats of bravery, some for their wisdom, some for their sanctity, some for outstanding integrity. But hero or sage, man or woman, all possessed a rare and indefinable natural quality: they generated a public feeling that they were touched by the hand of God. They had charisma, the emanation of divine grace, so that the respect and prestige they commanded cut across tribal boundaries.

Moses charged the people the same day, saying… these shall stand upon Mount Gerizim to bless the people… And these shall stand upon Mount Ebal for the curse

(Deuteronomy 27:12, 13)

Mount Ebal (left) and Mount Gerizim (below), the two mountains
above Shechem where Joshua, in the midst of his military campaign,
assembled his people for a religious ceremony in which he
solemnly read out the Laws handed down at Sinai. He also followed
the injunction of Moses (in Deuteronomy 27:12, 13)
to proclaim the blessings from the top of Gerizim and the
curses from the summit of Ebal. To this day, Mount Ebal is
bleak, while Mount Gerizim is green and fruitful.

the people of Israel assembled at Shiloh, and set up the tent of the meeting there; the land lay subdued before them (Joshua 18:1)

Ancient Hebrew writing on an ostracon (left),
an inscribed potsherd, found at archaeological
excavations a few miles south of Tel Aviv.
Remains of a cultic site in Shiloh (right). It was at Shiloh
that Joshua established the centre of worship for the
tribes of Israel, and it was to remain their religious
centre for the next two centuries, until it was
superseded by Jerusalem in the reign of king David.

When crisis came, there would be a general demand that they assume the leadership of the people.

THE CHARISMATIC TWELVE

Of the twelve Judges who appear in the Bible, six receive little more than a mention, so that we cannot follow the political and military pattern of their times, the enemies they faced or the exploits with which their leadership is associated. The six who figure more prominently in the biblical record, and were evidently the most outstanding, were Othniel, Ehud, Deborah, Gideon, Jephthah and Samson. Of these, Deborah and Gideon were undoubtedly the most important and Samson was the most colourful.

Othniel is the first of the warrior-Judges to be listed as having been "raised up" by the Lord as "a deliverer for the people of Israel" (Jud. 3:9), after they had been hard-pressed by a certain king Cushan-rishathaim. He led his people to war against the oppressor and was victorious; but the area of his operations and the strategy and tactics he used are not known. He is presumed to have been active

After these things Joshua the son of Nun, the servant of the Lord, died... And they buried him in his own inheritance at Timnath-serah, which is in the hill country of Ephraim. (Joshua 24:29, 30)

The death of Joshua. From an illuminated manuscript in the Pierpont Morgan collection.

at the beginning of the twelfth century.

He was followed by Ehud and we are told rather more about him. He belonged to the tribe of Benjamin, whose designated area of settlement lay between Judah, to the south, and Ephraim, to the north. In his day, the Israelites were feeling the pressure of the Moabites, who had secured control of the territory east of the Jordan and were penetrating westwards, across the river. With the help of "Ammon and Amalek" they reached "the city of palms" (Jud. 3:13) — Jericho — and put the local Israelites under tribute. It was at Jericho that Ehud carried out a daring individual deed which prepared the way for a successful military action — and liberation. Ostensibly bearing tribute to the king of Moab, he smuggled a dagger into the throne chamber, secured a private audience by a ruse, and slew the enemy ruler. (How Ehud got past the king's guards without being disarmed is well explained by Yigael Yadin in a fascinating examination of the clues in the biblical narrative. They are provided by such details as that Ehud was "left-handed" and made himself a sword with "two edges, of a cubit

اینجا جسوی جانرا سپرد و از عالم درگذشت

Valiter Iofue composito statu filiorum
Israhel moritur.

א רונות רחלות כדדן ידושע

Pilgrimage to the Western Wall of Temple Mount, again made possible by the re-unification of Jerusalem in 1967. In the time of Joshua and the Judges, Shiloh was the centre of pilgrimage; but after King David brought the Ark of the Law to Jerusalem in the 10th century BC, it was to Jerusalem that the "congregation of Israel" thronged to celebrate the three Pilgrim Festivals of Passover, Pentecost and Succoth.

Deborah, a prophetess... was judging Israel at that time. She used to sit under the palm of Deborah between Ramah and Bethel... (Judges 4:4, 5)

It was under a palm tree in the hill country of Ephraim that Deborah the Judge would sit and give counsel to the people of Israel. She played a decisive role in promoting unity among the tribes and at a time of critical danger spurred them to military victory.

length" — fifteen inches — which he fastened "under his raiment upon his right thigh". At that time the standard sword in the region was the large curved type, and the guards would not have failed to notice such a weapon. Describing it as two-edged clearly showed that it was a straight sword. It was short, little more than a dagger, and easy to hide. And telling us that it was fastened to his right side — because Ehud was left-handed — meant that in searching for weapons the king's guards would have missed it, paying attention only to the innocent left thigh.)

Having slain the king and departed, Ehud promptly hurried to the hill-country of Ephraim, sounded the alert, led the assembled force eastwards to the river Jordan and seized the fords. The Moabites on the west bank were cut off. Faced by this unexpected situation, and already confounded by the death of their king and commander, they fell an easy prey to the Israelites.

In the days of Jephthah, the enemy was Ammon, who had become the new master of Transjordan. Like their predecessors, the Ammonites too cast covetous eyes westwards,

Go, gather your men at Mount Tabor... And I will draw out Sisera, the general of Jabin's army... and I will give him into your hand (Judges 4:6, 7)

Mount Tabor (left), the hill in the valley of Jezreel, where Deborah urged the Israelite general Barak to assemble his forces and give battle to the army of Sisera, the commanding general of "Jabin king of Canaan". The archaeological site of biblical Megiddo (below), a few miles west of Mount Tabor and commanding a strategic pass at the western end of the valley of Jezreel, was close to the battlefield where the crucial clash took place.

The valley of Jezreel, as seen from the summit of Mount Tabor, looking south.

and hoped to take advantage of the tribal separatism of the Israelites. They began with probing harassment, followed this up with larger scale attacks, and overran land settled by the Israelites in Gilead (also in Transjordan, to the northwest of Ammon). It was then that the elders of Gilead sent for one of their sons, Jephthah, who had been driven from his home because his mother had been a prostitute, and who now resided in the land of Tob, northeast of Gilead, at the head of a band of Gileadites who had followed him. He returned with his own force, assembled the militiamen of Gilead and Manasseh, and led them all into battle against the Ammonites, routing their army and pursuing them into their own territory. The biblical account of his campaigns shows him to have been a formidable commander. (Jud. 11, 12.)

Samson was quite different. He did not command an army in battle, but acted rather as a one-man commando unit. He is perhaps the least "Judge-like" of all, for although he "judged Israel . . . twenty years", the account of his activities (Jud. 13–16) is less a record of leadership than of exciting deeds of legendary

206

The kings... fought... by the waters of Megiddo

(Judges 5:19)

The 9th century BC water tunnel of Megiddo, designed to give its inhabitants access to the fresh water spring outside the city walls even during siege. This tunnel was bored through the rock for a distance of 300 feet to the outside spring. The spring opening was camouflaged, so that it would be unnoticed by the besieging forces.

strength and daring. His period was the early part of the 11th century, when the neighbouring Philistines, energetic, aggressive and well-armed — they held the secret for manufacturing iron — were proving very troublesome to the Israelites. They conducted frequent border raids (which were ultimately to develop into all-out war). Samson single-handedly harried them, and the Bible offers colourful accounts of his exploits. He slew thirty Philistines in Ashkelon and took their spoil to pay for a wager he had lost through Philistine deceit. (Jud. 14:19.) He set fire to the standing corn and stooks, vineyards and olive groves of an immense area of Philistine land by tying firebrands to the tails of three hundred "foxes" (probably jackals) and setting them loose. (Jud. 15:5.) He slew a thousand of the enemy with the "jawbone of an ass." (Jud. 15:15.) And even at the moment of death, the blinded Samson shouted "Let me die with the Philistines" as he tore down the temple to Dagon with his bare hands. The multitude within were killed, and "the dead whom he slew at his death were more than those whom he had slain during his life."

Panoramic view of Zorah and Eshtaol, west of Jerusalem,
the region where Samson was born, spent his childhood
years, and developed the qualities of strength and daring which
were later to mark his legendary deeds against the Philistines.

the woman bore a son, and called his name Samson...
the boy grew... the Spirit of the Lord began to stir
him in Mahaneh-dan, between Zorah and Eshtaol

(Judges 13:24, 25)

The recently discovered water system of Gibeon (El Jib),
six miles northwest of Jerusalem. Archaeology has shown that
the Israelite settlement was responsible for the first intensive
development of the land, particularly of the hill country.
A key factor was their urgent concern with water conservation
and the construction of appropriate water installations.

At a time when his people's morale was low, Samson's derring-do unquestionably did much to raise Israelite spirits.

The impact of Deborah was of course far wider and deeper. She played a decisive role both in bringing about the defeat of the enemy and in promoting the unity of her people — though even she, while securing the ready response of several tribes, did not gain the support of all. The story of Deborah (Jud. 4.5) shows that at this early period — she lived in the second half of the 12th century BC, some 75 years before Samson — even when there was a grave threat from neighbouring enemies, some tribes who did not feel themselves in immediate danger failed to go to the help of their brothers. By now, several of the Canaanite groups who had not been subdued under Joshua had built up their strength and allied themselves under the banner of Sisera, the commanding general of "Jabin king of Canaan". Armed with chariots, which the Israelites lacked, they first sought to dominate the valley of Jezreel, which would have cut off the tribal areas in the centre of the country from those in Galilee, and had already sub-

then fought the kings of Canaan, at Ta'anach *(Judges 5:19)*

The ancient wall of Ta'anach in western Jezreel, unearthed in archaeological excavations. Ta'anach is mentioned with nearby Meggido in the Song of Deborah as the combat area where Barak battled with Sisera.

jugated some of the peripheral Israelite settlements. They now threatened to reach out north and south of this valley and crush the Israelites.

Deborah realised that this was the moment for all the tribes to join together to stop the enemy. She lived in the hill country of Ephraim, was much respected in her own tribe and had evidently gained wide renown as a sagacious, farsighted and very determined person. But she was not a military figure, and the situation called for an army commander. Apparently the outstanding Israelite soldier at the time was Barak, whose tribe of Naphtali were settled in upper Galilee, and Deborah sent for him. She urged him to mobilise the men of his and a neighbouring tribe and lead them in action. Barak agreed — on one condition: "If you will go with me, I will go; but if you will not go with me, I will not go." (Jud. 4:8.) This reply has been taken as a reflection of weakness and lack of self-assurance on the part of Barak, and he has been relegated to a minor role in the important battle which followed. Indeed, the Bible indicates that because of it, the glory of

212

The head of a Philistine anthropoid coffin of the 12th century BC discovered in archaeological excavations at Beth Shan, near the Jordan Valley.

slaying Sisera fell not to him but to a woman, Jael. But Barak was simply acting within the sphere of his competence. He was a general, not a popular leader, and he recognised that he lacked the moral influence to persuade the other tribes to go to war under his command. Only Deborah, by virtue of her charisma, could do that. She accordingly joined him in an appeal to the other tribes, and those who responded encamped at Mount Tabor against the enemy, the hilly ground offering some protection against the Canaanite chariot squadrons. One cannot tell whether Barak and Deborah timed the confrontation for the rainy season, but from the biblical account it is clear that heavy downpours had swollen a nearby river and robbed Sisera's forces of their principal advantage — mobility. Their chariots got bogged in the mud and the horse-drawn warriors proved a static prey to the charging Israelite foot-soldiers. The enemy was routed and the threat lifted from Israel.

In the immortal victory song of Deborah and Barak, there is high praise for the tribes who rallied to the colours — some, like Benjamin in the south and part of Manasseh

213

*the angel of the Lord came and sat under the oak...
which belonged to Joash... as his son Gideon was
beating out wheat in the wine press, to hide it from
the Midianites* (Judges 6:11)

Gideon was winnowing wheat when he
received the call which propelled him into
battle command and the subsequent
leadership of his people. In some Arab
villages of Israel today, the ancient methods
of separating the grain from the chaff
are still followed.

from across the Jordan, came from quite a
distance to take part in the fighting — and
withering scorn for those who stayed away.
"Zebulun is a people that jeoparded their lives
to the death; Naphtali too . .", but among
the clans of Reuben "there were great
searchings of heart. Why did you tarry among
the sheepfolds, to hear the piping for the
flocks?.. and Dan, why did he abide with the
ships? Asher sat still..!" Deborah's public
contempt for the tribes who failed to fight was
presumably intended to shame them into
action, if and when the House of Israel were
again threatened.

Gideon (Jud. 6–8), unlike Barak, was both
an inventive military commander and a
popular leader, so popular and successful,
indeed, that the people offered to make him
king, calling upon him to "rule over us". He
rejected the offer, saying "the Lord will rule
over you"; but it is already evident that the
tribes were beginning to think in terms of a
central administration. By this time—the 11th
century — the Israelites were prospering eco-
nomically. They were no longer novices at
farming. They had acquired the technique of

building. And they had put to good use the discovery of lime plaster for lining cisterns. Water storage now enabled the hill country to support a denser population, and forests were cleared to make possible the cultivation and settlement of land which had hitherto been bare of people. Their prosperity was an inviting temptation to their neighbours — both immediate and distant — and this no doubt led them to thoughts of cooperation under a national leader. They would get such a leader a few decades later.

The particular problem that afflicted them in the time of Gideon were the annual raids at harvest time from the camel-riding Midianites who came up from the southern desert and across the Jordan. This had been going on for several years, the attackers gaining fresh encouragement and confidence with each victory, and threatened ruin to Israel. Gideon, of the tribe of Manasseh, resolved to take action, and the next time a large horde of Midianites crossed the Jordan and brazenly encamped in the valley of Jezreel, Gideon rallied the men of his own clan and of neighbouring clans and gathered stealthily at the spring of Harod just opposite the tents of the enemy. There he proceeded with his celebrated "water" test, choosing only three hundred picked men and sending the rest home. He then carried out a personal reconnaissance patrol at night, accompanied only by his aide Purah, and got close enough to the Midianite guards to hear them talking. From the intelligence he gathered, he devised a stratagem, briefed his men and soon put it into operation. He equipped each of his three hundred troops with a trumpet, a torch hidden inside a pitcher, and a sword, and he formed them into three companies. They then crept up to the outskirts of the sleeping enemy encampment in the middle of the night and the three companies positioned themselves on three sides of the bivouac area. The fourth side, the east, was left unattended. Gideon waited until the change of guard of "the middle watch" had been completed. Then, before the new shift of drowsy Midianite guards had the chance to rub the sleep from their eyes, Gideon gave the signal — a trumpet blast — and his three hundred men followed suit, blowing their trumpets, smashing their pitchers with the torches against the enemy tents and setting them ablaze, and shouting "A sword for the Lord and for Gideon". The panic-stricken Midianites, taken by surprise, utterly confused by the din and made frantic by the fire, ran helter-skelter. Those who rushed through the perimeter of flame in a mad race for safety were met by the swords of Gideon's men. The main body fled through the un-guarded east side, towards the Jordan river, as Gideon had planned. He now sent urgent messages to the other tribes to dash towards the river Jordan to meet and deal with the fleeing Midianites, and he himself set off in pursuit. The victory was complete.

It was so dramatic that Gideon, whose valour had been known only to the clans of his tribe, was now acclaimed as a national hero. Moreover, his initial rout of the enemy with only three hundred men showed, as it was designed to show, that deliverance had come from the Lord. Gideon was thus seen to be the instrument of God, and it was then that the tribes agreed to offer him the leader-ship of the people. "And the land had rest forty years in the days of Gideon."

The period of the Judges, from the beginning of the 12th to the latter part of the 11th century BC, covering the years of settlement following the Joshua conquest, was an agonizing period of transition during which the fate of the Israelites and of their religion hung frequently in the balance. There were times when it was questionable whether the tribes would survive or go under; whether they would retain their unique identity or assimilate into the surrounding peoples; whether they would remain faithful to their Covenant and their Commandments or adopt the gods of their neighbours.

Only with the emergence of the Prophet Samuel, who pulled the tribes together and gave them central direction and leadership, do we find Israel launched on its crucial voyage of creative development. Under Samuel's successors, the kings Saul, David and Solomon, Israel rose to its greatest glory. And it was the Prophets, the visionaries and poets of the following five turbulent centuries, who consolidated the unique historic works initiated by Moses, giving permanent form to the Jewish religion and to Jewish nationhood.

Jerubba'al (that is, Gideon) and all the people who were with him rose early and encamped beside the spring of Harod (Judges 7:1)

The Spring of Harod in the valley of Jezreel, where Gideon
conducted his celebrated "water test" and selected 300 picked
men from among the thousands who had volunteered.
With this small force he carried out a commando attack
at night on the huge Midianite army which had
penetrated Jezreel and encamped opposite
Harod. The Midianites were routed.
The Spring of Harod is now a National Park.

219

A

Aaron, brother of Moses, 41, 44, 49, 57, 58, 60, 65, 76, 77, 80, 102, 105, 133, 137, 140, 144, 145, 154; meets Pharaoh, 68; and golden calf, 134; ordained as priest, 139; death of, 160

Abiram, revolt of, 154

Abu Rudeis, 92, 102

Abu Augeila, 87

Ai, 180, 187; abortive assault on. 178; conquest by Joshua, 180

Aijalon, Valley of, 180, 185

Ain el Kudeirat (Kadesh Barnea), 89

Albright, William Foxwell, 190, 194

Alt, Albrecht, 121

Amalekites, 108, 141, 147; attack Israelit rearguard, 105; tactics, 105, in Negev, 144; allied with Moabites, 200

Amenemhat, Egyptian chief of works, 24, 28

Ammon, 160, 194; allied with Moab, 200; defeated by Jephthah, 203

Amorites, 144; refuse passage to Israelites, 160

Amram, father of Moses, 21

Anak, 144

Apis, sacred bull of Egypt, 136

Aqaba, 37

Arabian desert, 105

Aramaeans, 194

Arnon, river, 158, 160

Asher, tribe of, 140, 214

Ashkelon, 209

Assyrian law, 129, 130, 133

Avaris, founded by Hyksos, 12, 17; razed by Egyptians, 16; city of stores built on its site and renamed Raamses, 17, 65; see also Tanis and Zoan

B

Babylonian law, 127, 133

Balaam, soothsayer with reluctant ass, 160

Balak, king of Moab, 160

Barak, Deborah's general, 212, 213, 214

Bardawil, Lake, 85, 87, 89

Beersheba, 89, 143

Benjamin, tribe of, 140, 200, 213

Bethel, 135, 178, 190

Beth Horon, 185

Bitter Lakes, Great and Little, 89, 92

Bright, John, 117, 171

C

Caleb, optimistic member of 12-spy team; 145; consulted by Moses, 145, 147; one of three Exodus survivors, 160

Canaan, the Promised Land, 9, 12, 85, 127, 143, 147, 154, 155, 158, 188; twelve spies reconnoitre, 143–145; Moses views, 164; conquest of, 169–186

Commandments, the Ten, 112–133
Constantine, Roman emperor, 92
Covenant Code and Covenant Treaties, 117–133

D

Dagon, temple of, 209
Damascus, 155, 185
Dan, tribe of, 135, 140, 141, 214
Dathan, revolt of, 151
David, 188
Dead Sea, 155, 164, 168, 172
Debir, 185, 187; see also Kiriath-Sepher and Tel Beit Mirsim
Deborah, Judge, 195, 199, 211; rallies tribes, 212; sends general Barak against Sisera, 213; Song of, 214

E

Ebal, Mount of the Curse, 187
Edom, 158; refuses passage to Israelites, 155
Eglon, 183, 185
Egypt: dominant power, 9, 11; Hyksos overrun, 12, 16; Hebrews in, 9–76; Exodus from, 77
Ehud, Judge, 199, 200; slays Moabite king, 203
Eilat, Gulf of, 155
El Arish, 85
Eliezer, son of Moses, 49
Elim, 101, 102; see also Wadi Firan
Ephraim, tribe of, 105, 140, 141, 144, 188, 200, 203
Etham, 79
Etzion Geber, 155

F

Frontinus, 176

G

Gad, tribe of, 140, 188
Galilee, 12, 185, 211
Gerizim, Mount of the Blessing, 187

Gershom, son of Moses, 49
Gezer, 185, 186
Gibeon, 180, 183, 185
Gideon, Judge, 199, 214, 216; conducts "water test", 216; defeats Midianites, 216, 217
Gilead, 160, 206
Gilgal, 172, 180, 183
Golan Heights, 160
Goshen, Land of, 11, 12, 16, 17, 53, 74
Greenberg, Moshe, 129, 133

H

Haggada of Passover, 77
Hammurabi, Babylonian king: Code of, 127, 133
Harod, Spring of, 216
Hazor: conquest by Joshua, 185; archaeological excavations at, 12, 186
Hebron, 144, 183, 185
Heshbon, 158, 160
Hitler, 19
Hittite: empire, 9, 18; people, 147; covenant treaties of, 117, 118; Code of, 127, 130
Hor, Mount, burial place of Aaron, 160
Horeb, Mount (Mount Sinai), 40, 41, 108
Huleh Valley, 185
Hur, 105, 133
Hyksos: overrun Egypt, 12; archaeological remains of, 12; patrons of Joseph, 16

I

Ibn Ezra, 147
Isaac, 40
Ismailia, 17, 79
Israel, 12, 16, 58, 65, 77, 105, 117, 119, 160, 164, 187, 190, 213
Issachar, tribe of, 140

J

Jabbok, river, 160
Jabin, "king of Canaan", 211

Jacob, 11, 40, 53, 160

Jael, slayer of Sisera, 213

Jarmuth, 183

Jebel Hilel, 87

Jebel Libne, 87

Jebel Mussa, 92

Jebusites, 144

Jephthah, Judge, 195; defeats Ammorites 203, 206

Jericho, 158, 164, 180; spies in, 172; conquest by Joshua, 176; archaeological excavations at, 187; Ehud slays Moabite king in, 200

Jeroboam, 135

Jerusalem, 164, 183, 185, 186, 188

Jethro (Reuel), father-in-law of Moses, 37, 41, 44, 49, 96, 161; advises Moses on administrative reforms, 108, 109, 136

Jezreel, Valley of, 211, 216

Jochebed, mother of Moses, 21, 23

Jordan, river, 144, 158, 160, 164, 168, 176, 188, 194, 200, 203, 214, 217

Joseph, 11, 16, 188

Joshua: summoned by Moses, 105; first battle, 105; accompanies Moses to Mount Sinai, 134; reconnaissance mission as one of twelve spies, 144–147; train army, 154; one of three Exodus survivors, 160; succeeds Moses, 164; campaigns in Canaan, 168–186; archaeological discoveries at sites he conquered, 186–187; establishes centre of worship at Shloh, 188; confirms covenant tradition at Shechem, 190; death of, 191

Judah, tribe of 140, 141, 145, 188

Justinian I, Roman emperor, 92

K

Kadesh Barnea, 89, 92, 105, 127; Israelites reach, and stay thirty-eight years, 141–154; see also Ain el-Kudeirat

Kantara, 85

Kiriath-Sepher, 187, 190, see also Debir

Korah, revolt of, 151

Kuseima, 89

L

Lachish, 183, 185, 187

Lebanon, 186

Libnah, 185

Levites, priestly tribe, 140, 151

M

Makkedah, 185

Manasseh, tribe of, 140, 188, 206, 213

Manzala, Lake, 17

Marah, 95, 96 101, 102

"Massah and Meribah", 105

Mediterranean, 85, 87

Mendenhall, George, 118, 119, 121, 124, 127

Merom, 185

Mesopotamia, 85, 155

Michelangelo, 137, 139

Midian, 37, 160, 194, 216

Miriam, sister of Moses, 23, 40, 41; palace meetings with Moses, 31; leads victory dance, 95; death of, 154

Moab, 155, 158, 160, 168, 194, 200, 203

Montet, Pierre, 74

Moses, 9; birth, 21; found by princess, 23; at court of Pharaoh, 24–32; with Jethro in the desert, 32–40; revelation at burning bush, 40; returns to rally his people, 44–65; encounters with Pharaoh, 65–77; leads Exodus, 79–110; receives Decalogue on Mount Sinai, 112–124; enacts ordinances, 124–133; develops nation-building in Kadesh, 151–154; leaves Kadesh and leads fighting-march to east bank of Jordan, 154–160; farewell address, 160–164; death of, 168

Mycenaean pottery, archaeological evidence of date of Joshua's conquest, 186

N

Naphtali, tribe of, 140, 214
Nebo, Mount, where Moses viewed future Land of Israel, 164, 168
Negev, 144, 148, 155
Nile, river, 21, 41, 74, 76, 80

O

Og, king of Bashan, 160, 176
Othniel, Judge, 199

P

Passover (Pesah), Festival of Freedom, 76, 77, 172
Philistines, 85, 89, 194, 209
Pisgah, 164
Phithom, 17
Plagues, the Ten, 74–77
Port Said, 17
Port Taufiq, 92

R

Raamses, 17, 65; also see Avaris
Rahab, 172
Rameses I, 17
Rameses II, the Pharaoh at the time of the Exodus, 17, 65
Ras Sudar, 92
Reed Sea ("Red Sea"), 79, 80, 84, 89
Rephidim, 104, 105, 108, 154
Reuben, tribe of, 140, 141, 188, 214
Reuel, see also Jethro, 37

S

Samson, Judge, 199, 206, 209
Saul, 217
Sethos I, the Pharaoh at the time of Moses' birth, 17
Shechem, 187, 188, 190

Shiloh: centre of worship established by Joshua, 188, 195; tribal centre, 191
Shur, wilderness of, 95
Sihon, king of the Amorites, 158, 160, 176
Simeon, tribe of, 140
Sinai, Mount, where the Israelites received the Ten Commandments, 112–133
Sisera, Canaanite general, 211, 213
Solomon, 217
S. Pietro in Vincoli, Church of, 137
St. Catherine's Monastery, 192;
Succoth, Festival of Tabernacles, 190; place name, 79
Suez, canal, 11, 89; Gulf of, 92, 102
Syria, 12, 186, 194

T

Tabor, Mount, 213
Tanis, 17; see also Avaris
Tel Beit Mirsim, 190; see also Debir and Kiriath-Sepher
Timsah, Lake, 17
Tob, 206
Transjordan, 155, 188, 203

W

Wadi Firan, 92, 102; see also Elim
Wadi Hammamat, 24
Weinfeld, Moshe, 118, 119, 135, 190
Wellhausen, Julius, 117

Y

Yadin, Yigael, 12, 176, 186, 200
Yarmuk, river, 160

Z

Zebulun, tribe of, 140, 214
Zin, wilderness of, 148
Zoan, 17; see also Avaris

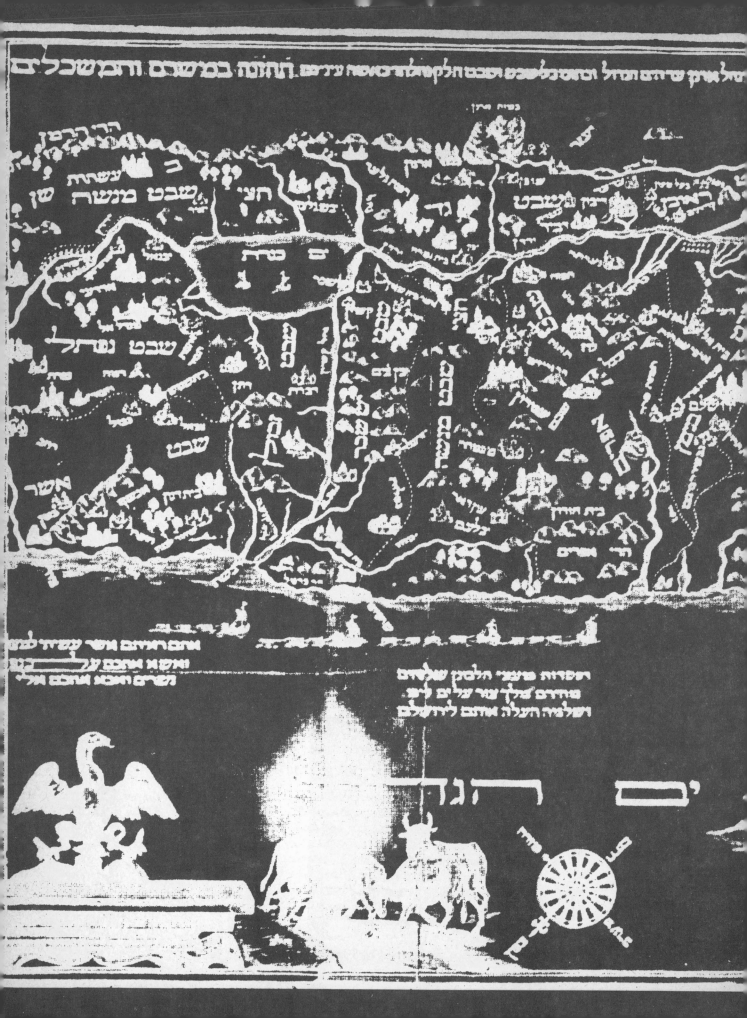